Collins

Revised Tune In!

Master Your Listening and Speaking Skills

Adheres to National Education Policy
MIDDLE STAGE

Author: Dr Sherin Shervani | **Series Editor:** Dr K Padmini Shankar

Preface

Revised Tune In! is an innovative listening and speaking course that is closely aligned with the National Education Policy, 2020. The course consists of eight books for Classes 1 to 8 with their accompanying audio-visual resources.

Aims

The main aim of *Revised Tune In!* is to help students gain communicative competence in using English in the real world by developing the key aural and oral skills. It aids to boost confidence in learners to develop fluency in using English in academic, personal and social contexts. It uses a step-by-step interactive approach with experiential tasks based on 21st century skills to help learners listen, understand and respond appropriately.

The number of chapters ranges from 10 to 13 in each level. Each chapter is built around a theme and focuses on specific language and communicative functions related to it. Special focus is also given on enriching the fund of context-specific vocabulary and spoken grammar, along with the use of correct pronunciation, intonation, stress and pause.

The chapters are structured to include the following sections:

Learning objectives defines language learning goals at the beginning of each chapter.

Getting started introduces the theme in an engaging way.

Listening and learning includes focused listening activities that help learners develop active listening skills, scan for details and draw inferences from what they have heard.

Speaking and practising has focused speaking activities that help learners develop fluency and accuracy in speaking, and hone their presentation skills.

Saying it right covers different aspects of phonics and pronunciation.

Word Wizard provides vocabulary support in the form of key words and phrases required for the task.

Grammar Guide provides language and grammar inputs to facilitate accurate language production.

Manners matter! contains gestural and verbal clues that are vital for making the right impression while speaking.

Info byte provides quick tips and tricks about sounds and spoken language.

Interacting and communicating includes integrated listening and speaking tasks; usually interactive pair and group work for students to practise and assess what they have learnt.

Fun Activity contains activities for enjoyment while learning.

Each book also has the following special features:

Dictation time provides additional practice for the learners' listening and spelling skills.

Take a break! are three well-designed activities that allow learners to refresh the topics learnt in the preceding chapters.

Saying it better! teaches common phrases and guides learners to avoid incorrect and colloquial language usage.

Children's Literary Fest is an art-integrated activity that focuses on increasing the learners' interest in literature.

How to use the book

Each chapter is based on a theme and focuses on a communicative function. Parents and teachers can initiate the learners into the theme of the chapter through the warm-up activity given in *Getting started*.

Chapter

Draw the student's attention to the learning objectives given at the beginning of the chapters. This would help them to focus on the key learning points of the chapter.

Do the listening and learning activities for developing active listening skills. Play the audio tracks at least twice for 'while-listening' and 'post-listening' tasks. During the first time, the students should be asked only to listen. When they listen to it for the second time, get them to complete the task. Give them clear instructions at the beginning of the tasks and check whether they understand what needs to be done.

Conduct the phonic drills and pronunciation activities with care. Get the students to listen and repeat the words and phrases multiple times till they get the pronunciation right. While this can be done as a class activity too, it would be best to monitor each student individually. Use the audio-visual input to learn the right way of making the English sounds.

When conducting the speaking activities, make sure all the students get a fair chance to participate. Demonstrate the task and check whether the students know how to do it. The presentation tips given for the activities in the *Manners matter!* boxes can be used to inculcate good habits and to build the right attitude required in students to make an impression when they speak.

For Assessment

Teachers can choose any of the listening and speaking activities for testing the students' achievement levels. It is, however, advisable to share the parameters of assessment with the students beforehand so that they know what is expected of them. Teachers can refer to the Teacher's Resource Books for this.

Teacher's Resource Books contain the lesson plans, teaching strategies and the answer keys besides the parameters of assessment for each task.

DigiSuite, the interactive digital resource pack, has the e-book with audio for the listening tasks, interactive activities and training videos demonstrating the right way of doing the speaking tasks.

We hope that teachers and students would find this series useful in developing listening and pronunciation and speaking skills and that it would enable students to become effective communicators in English.

Key to NEP tags and SDG icons

Revised Tune In! is a listening and speaking course that is closely aligned with the National Education Policy, 2020. It uses interactive approach and experiential activities to build communicative competence in students. This series aims to prepare learners with the various skills outlined in the National Education Policy, 2020.

These skills have been tagged appropriately for the user's convenience. Here is the key to the tags.

India Focus NEP

- India Focus puts spotlight on the heritage, culture, customs, and history and geography of the Indian subcontinent.
- This provides students a deeper understanding of their homeland and creates a sense of solidarity.

Art Integration NEP

- Art Integrated Learning (AIL) is a teaching-learning model that integrates fine arts (painting, sculpture, architecture, music, and poetry), performing arts (theatre and dance), and photography with teaching new concepts.
- This provides students with an experiential and a multi-disciplinary learning experience.

Cross-curricular NEP

- The cross-curricular approach to a topic recognizes that all subjects are interlinked. It includes contributions from several different disciplines or viewpoints for effective learning.
- Certain activities cover cross-curricular content appropriate to that class.

Happiness Content NEP

- Learning should be an enjoyable process for learners. It should focus on building and understanding new concepts rather than rote learning.
- Children should experience happiness through learning and awareness, active participation in class, and also in their relationships with their friends and family.

Experiential Learning NEP

- Experiential learning is a process of learning through hands-on experience. Here, students 'learn by doing' an activity followed by reflective observation on the experience from multiple perspectives.
- This method helps learners link existing knowledge to understand new concepts and apply it to make decisions.

Twenty-First Century Skills

- The twenty-first century skills ensure that today's students can thrive in an ever-changing world and can use these skills to learn constantly.
- Here are the most commonly cited twenty-first century skills in this series:

Critical Thinking NEP

Communication Skills NEP

Collaboration NEP

Creativity NEP

Digital Literacy NEP

Sustainable Development Goals

- The Sustainable Development Goals, adopted by the United Nations in 2015, are a collection of 17 interlinked global goals designed to achieve a better and more sustainable future for all by 2030.
- Here are the 17 goals:

1 NO POVERTY
2 ZERO HUNGER
3 GOOD HEALTH AND WELL-BEING
4 QUALITY EDUCATION
5 GENDER EQUALITY
6 CLEAN WATER AND SANITATION
7 AFFORDABLE AND CLEAN ENERGY
8 DECENT WORK AND ECONOMIC GROWTH
9 INDUSTRY, INNOVATION AND INFRASTRUCTURE
10 REDUCED INEQUALITIES
11 SUSTAINABLE CITIES AND COMMUNITIES
12 RESPONSIBLE CONSUMPTION AND PRODUCTION
13 CLIMATE ACTION
14 LIFE BELOW WATER
15 LIFE ON LAND
16 PEACE, JUSTICE AND STRONG INSTITUTIONS
17 PARTNERSHIPS FOR THE GOALS

Detailed Contents

Chapter	Listening and learning	Speaking and practising	Saying it right & Dictation time	Interacting and communicating	Fun Activity
1. **Casual greetings** (*Communicative functions:* informal greetings and leave-taking)	Listening to conversations for details and filling gaps; choosing correct options to complete the sentences	*Pair work:* enacting a situation between two friends meeting and greeting each other; *pair work:* practising informal greetings and their responses	Listening to and sorting words with *p* and *b* sounds and *t* and *th* sounds; listening to sentences and identifying unstressed words Listening to a passage and writing it down	*Pair work:* practising a conversation between two friends	*Group work:* playing dumb charades by enacting a given activity
2. **Introductions** (*Communicative functions:* introducing oneself and one's friends)	Choosing correct greetings; listening to conversations and filling gaps; identifying statements as true or false	*Group work:* imagining oneself as a different person and then introducing oneself to a group, as per the descriptions provided	Practising and sorting words with *d* and *th* sounds; practising words with *ack*, *all*, *ank* and *ash* sounds and writing rhyming words Listening to a passage and writing it down	*Pair work:* interviewing one's partner and introducing him/her to the class	*Group work:* playing finish-the-story game with a few given prompts
3. **Talking about school** (*Communicative functions:* talking about school and responsibilities at school; sharing learning; asking and answering questions; expressing one's feelings and points of view about something)	Listening for details and choosing correct options	*Group work:* discussing pictures based on questionnaires; *pair work:* asking and answering questions about each other provided in the questionnaires	Listening to similar-sounding words and circling the correct answers; practising sentences with similar-sounding words Listening to a passage and writing it down	*Group work:* discussing how educated people can share their knowledge with others; suggesting ways of making school a better place	*Group work:* discussing class rules in groups and making a poster on them
Take a break!					
4. **Our community** (*Communicative functions:* talking about community responsibilities; making plans to do something for the society; excusing oneself from doing something and accepting others' refusal)	Listening for details and completing a flyer; listening to a radio appeal and choosing the correct words; listening to a conversation and identifying statements as true or false	*Pair work:* reading a passage on selfless service, discussing actionable charity work for people and animals; *group work:* discussing ways to raise money for a noble cause	Listening to and sorting words with two different *th* sounds; listening to and sorting words ending with *ill*, *ing* and *ink* Listening to a passage and writing it down	*Role-play:* expressing one's inability to participate in a charity programme and accepting others' refusal politely	*Group work:* discussing ways of making the lives of elderly people safer and better
5. **Shopping on the go** (*Communicative functions:* ordering food and things over the phone or the Internet; exploring solutions to problems faced when shopping or buying things over the phone or the Internet)	Listening to conversations for details and choosing correct options; identifying statements as true or false	*Pair work:* role-playing ordering food at a restaurant over the phone; *group work:* discussing solutions to different problems faced when shopping or using online services	Practising words beginning with the *f* sound; listening to and sorting words with *ock*, *uck*, *ump* and *unk* sounds; listening to and practising correct intonation Listening to a passage and writing it down	Conducting a survey on the use of apps and presenting the results in the class	*Pair work:* playing dumb charades to enact a shopping scene
6. **At the bank** (*Communicative functions:* talking about banking and opening an account; discussing financial management)	Listening to a conversation for details and choosing correct options; listening for details to a description of mobile banking and filling gaps	*Pair work:* role-playing a conversation for filling out a deposit slip; *pair work:* discussing a plan to save money for a special occasion	Listening for details and filling gaps; listening to and sorting words with *ee* and *oo* sounds; *pair work:* practising a dialogue Listening to a passage and writing it down	*Pair work:* role-playing a conversation to practise using the right tones; role-playing a conversation about a banking problem	Thinking of some practical ways of earning money and sharing them with the class
Take a break!					
7. **My dreams** (*Communicative functions:* talking about one's dreams and ambitions; discussing possibilities and probabilities)	Listening to definitions for details and matching sentence parts; listening to a poem for details and filling gaps	*Group work:* listening to a poem and asking and answering questions based on it; *pair work:* asking and answering questions about each other's goals in life	Practising pauses in sentences by using commas and semicolons in sentences Listening to a passage and writing it down	Delivering a speech as a famous person	Asking parents and grandparents about their childhood ambitions and their fulfilment

Chapter	Listening and learning	Speaking and practising	Saying it right & Dictation time	Interacting and communicating	Fun Activity
8. **Let's party** (*Communicative functions:* inviting, accepting and refusing invitations politely; offering food/drinks and accepting/declining such offers; complimenting someone and accepting compliments with gratitude)	Listening for details and filling gaps; listening to invitations and their responses and choosing the correct options	*Pair work:* learning to extend invitations for different events and responding to them; *group work:* role-playing a birthday party situation to practice offering, accepting and refusing food	Listening to and sorting words with soft *c* and hard *c* sounds; listening to a recipe and punctuating it with commas and semi-colons Listening to a passage and writing it down	*Pair work:* practicising complimenting your classmates	Making an invitation card
9. **Entertainment** (*Communicative functions:* expressing opinions about films and TV shows; answering questions on the basis of listening; booking tickets over the telephone)	Listening to conversations for details and choosing correct options and filling gaps	*Group work:* discussing a film or a TV programme; expressing one's views about a film or a TV programme and politely agreeing or disagreeing with others	Listening to and sorting words with three different *i* sounds; Listening to and sorting words with soft *g* and hard *g* sounds Listening to a passage and writing it down	Listening to a telephonic conversation for details and filling gaps; *pair work:* role-playing the conversation with your partner	Discussing one's favourite e-sport and making an advertisement poster on it
Take a break!					
10. **Getting our point across** (*Communicative functions:* learning to give and follow directions; learning to complete dialogues and interrupting speakers politely; learning to disagree politely)	Listening for details to mark directions and destinations on a map and filling gaps; listening for information and filling gaps	*Pair work:* asking for and giving directions to different places; role-playing a situation to justify one's request with proper reasons	Listening to and sorting words with two different *a* sounds; listening to and writing words ending with *ough* Listening to a passage and writing it down	*Pair work:* role-playing different situations to practise interrupting speakers politely	*Group work:* giving directions to a blindfolded group mate; reaching a destination blindfolded after listening to directions
11. **Science and technology** (*Communicative functions:* expressing one's views and opinions; ordering events on the basis of listening; comparing and contrasting situations; debating about environmental changes)	Listening to a news story for details and filling gaps; listening to a biographical passage and ordering the sentences correctly	*Pair work:* comparing and discussing life in older and modern times; *group work:* debating on a given topic	Listening to and sorting words with the diagraph *oo* and the diphthong *ow*; and words with short *o* and long *o* sounds Listening to a passage and writing it down	*Pair work:* watching a PowerPoint presentation on global warming and asking and answering questions on the subject	*Group work:* researching creative ways to recycle plastic waste and making a PowerPoint presentation on it
12. **What's in store for us?** (*Communicative functions:* expressing concern and distress; expressing one's anxiety and frustration; expressing satisfaction; evaluating the results of an action/event)	Listening to a speech for information and filling gaps; listening to a poem and writing it down	*Group work:* reading and discussing a passage on wildlife and delivering a speech on the subject; *pair work:* discussing environmental problems and suggesting solutions to tackle them	Listening to sentences and circling the correct forms of words; listening for words and writing them correctly Listening to a passage and writing it down	Listening to a news story and holding a class discussion on different ways of disposing waste in India, their advantages and disadvantages	Listening to Severn Suzuki's complete speech and expressing one's views about it
13. **Arts and crafts** (*Communicative functions:* talking about different arts and crafts; discussing ways of promoting dying Indian crafts)	Listening to instructions on making a Rajasthani puppet and ordering sentences correctly; listening to a radio announcement for details and filling in a brochure	*Group work:* reading an article and giving a presentation on the ways of promoting dying Indian crafts; *pair work:* asking and answering questions about arts and crafts	Listening to words to divide them into syllables; practising similar-sounding words and underlining the correct words Listening to a passage and writing it down	Visiting an arts and crafts fair or a handicraft unit and writing and presenting a report on it	Decorating the classroom with works of art, then organising an exhibition to show the artworks to students of other classes
Saying it better!					
Children's Literary Fest					

Contents

1 Casual greetings

In this chapter, we will:

- learn to greet people.
- listen to common expressions and choose the correct ones.
- learn to distinguish between the t and th sounds and the b and p sounds.
- learn to distinguish between the stressed and unstressed words in sentences.
- learn to sing with the correct rhythm, intonation and tone.

Getting started

Collaboration NEP

A. *Discuss* **Read this conversation between Sachin and Sahil. Then, work with a partner and discuss the greetings used by the two boys.**

Sachin: Hi, Sahil! Long time no see.

Sahil: Hi, Sachin! Yeah, it's been a while. How are you?

Sachin: I am pretty well. How about you?

Sahil: I'm fine too. Sorry, I need to run an errand for my mother right now. Let's catch up later.

Sachin: Sure! Let's meet on Sunday afternoon.

Sahil: Perfect! See you on Sunday afternoon then.

Sachin: Bye!

Listening and learning

B1. *Gap-fill*

1.1

Listen to a conversation between Sudhir and Deepa and complete the dialogue.

5 GENDER EQUALITY

Sudhir: Hello, Deepa! Long time .... Where have you been?

Deepa: Hello, Sudhir! How are you? Yes, I have been busy recently. My family is moving to ....

Sudhir: I see. Have you got transferred there?

Deepa: Yes. I have been promoted to a senior position in .... My family decided to move with me.

Sudhir: Congratulations! When are you shifting?

Deepa: I must join the the new office on 1st December, so we plan to reach Kochi .... before that.

Sudhir: Okay. All the best, Deepa!

Deepa: Thank you, Sudhir! I should go now. I need to do a lot of things.

Sudhir: Ok, ...!

Deepa: Bye!

B2. *Choose*

Listen to some common expressions we use when we meet our friends. Then, tick (✓) the correct expressions.

1. Hi, my name is Pakhi. It's ....!
   (nice to meet you/nice to meeting you)
2. It's good to see you! How ....?
   (is the thing/are things)
3. I missed you! Long ....!
   (time no seen/time no see)
4. Say .... (hello to/hello with) Sasha for me.
   I haven't seen her for a long time.
5. Piya, I haven't seen you for a long time. How ....
   ....? (you are doing/have you been)
6. Hi, Manan! It's .... (ok to see you/good to see you) after such a long time. Do you come to this gym daily?

Speaking and practising

Creativity NEP

C1. *Role-play*

Work in pairs. Imagine that you are meeting one of your school friends after several years. You are very happy to see him/her. Enact the situation.

Grammar Guide: Interesting language points

Here are some of the expressions we use when we meet friends:

How are you doing?	*How have you been?*
It's been so long!	*Long time no see!*
How is everything?	*How are things?*
It's so good to see/meet you!	*What have you been doing?*

C2. *Practise*

Work with a partner and practise the following expressions. First, read them out, then practise saying them without using the book.

Informal greetings

Hi, how's life?	Hi! How's everything?
Hey! What's new?	It's good to see you!

Responses

Great! What about yours?	Everything's fine. Thanks.
Nothing much. What about you?	Same here. How are you?

Saying it right

D1. *Sort* 1.3

Listen to some words, repeat them and write them in the correct columns.

Words with the **b** sound	Words with the **p** sound

D2. *Sort* 1.4

Listen and repeat the words correctly. Also, put the words in the correct columns.

Words with the **t** sound	Words with the **th** sound

D3. *Say aloud* 1.5

Listen to the sentences. Then say them aloud. Which of the words in these sentences are unstressed?

1. Mum and Dad went back to Delhi after the wedding. Sadly, the rest of the family met with an accident on the way.
2. Mum's from Orissa, Dad's from Chennai. We are a family of four and I have a sister, who stays with my aunt.

Dictation time

E. *Listen and write*

DT

Listen to the passage and write it in your notebook. Then, take turns to read it out to your partner.

Interacting and communicating

F. *Role-play*

1.6

Listen to the following conversation. Then, work with a partner and practise it.

Parul: Hello, Raveena! It's nice to catch up with you after such a long time.

Raveena: Hello, Parul! The pleasure is mine.

Parul: I think we should go out for lunch some day.

Raveena: That would be great.

Parul: What place do you suggest?

Raveena: How about Big Tummy?

Parul: That sounds good.

Raveena: All right. Does Saturday suit you?

Parul: Yes, that's fine.

Raveena: Okay, catch you later then. Bye!

Parul: Bye!

Fun Activity

Art Integration NEP

Divide the class into two teams. The first team will write a situation on a slip of paper. One person from the second team must mime it. The rest of the team members must guess within two minutes what is being mimed.

Take turns to mime and ensure that each of you get a chance to participate.

Here are some suggestions:

- You unexpectedly meet an old friend at a shop.
- You are knitting while sitting in a fast-moving train.
- You are eating spaghetti with chopsticks.
- You are a clumsy waiter.
- You are washing a big, angry dog.
- You are sweeping leaves on your lawn but on a windy day.
- You are dancing in the rain.
- You are helping your mother cook noodles.
- You are taking leave of your grandparents.

Each correct guess earns a point for your team. The team which earns the most points wins!

2 Introductions

In this chapter, we will:

- learn to introduce ourselves correctly.
- learn to introduce someone else to a group.
- learn to interview people.
- learn to differentiate between the d sound and the th sound.
- learn to say words ending with ack, all, ank and ash.

Getting started

A. *Guess* — **Take turns to tell your classmates two truths and one lie about you. Your classmates will guess which statements are true and which one is a lie.**

Listening and learning

B1. *Identify*

When you meet people for the first time, what do you say to greet them? Underline the correct option.

1. Hi, myself Sachin!/Hi, I am Sachin!
2. Hello, who are you?/Hello, how are you?
3. What to do?/What do you do?
4. Where are you in?/Where are you from?
5. It's nice in meeting you./It's nice to meet you.

B2. *Gap-fill*

2.1

Listen to a conversation between three friends. Fill in each blank with the name of the correct person.

1. .... introduces John and Anna to each other.
2. .... is from Mumbai.
3. .... is from Kerala.

B3. *Listen and write*

2.2

Listen again and complete the conversation.

1. Ruma: Hi, John! ....
2. John: Hi, Ruma! I'm fine. ....

3. Ruma: I'm fine too. ....
....

4. John: Hi, Anna! ....
....

5. Anna: Hi, John! ....
....

6. John: Where are you from, Anna?

7. Anna: I'm from Mumbai. ....
....

8. John: I'm ....

B4. *True or false* (2.3)

Listen to Aditya introduce Bhaskar to his school friends. Listen carefully and mark each statement as true (T) or false (F).

1. Aditya and Bhaskar first met when they were both six years old. ☐
2. Aditya and Bhaskar are brothers. ☐
3. Bhaskar now lives in Patna. ☐
4. Bhaskar has an older sister. ☐
5. Aditya and his friends like to play cricket. ☐
6. Bhaskar likes to listen to music. ☐
7. Bhaskar cooks well. ☐
8. Bhaskar wants to be an engineer when he grows up. ☐

Speaking and practising

Art Integration NEP

C. *Introduce*

Work in groups of five. Imagine that you are at a party and you are introducing yourself to the other guests. Assume the identity of one of the persons described in the table and then introduce yourself.

Akshita Bhatia Sales Manager at BCL Books; lives in Mumbai; likes to travel and read books	**Saurav Bhalla** Doctor at a government hospital; lives in Bhopal; lung specialist; likes to exercise and listen to music
Uday Rao Engineer with TEFL companies; lives in Ranchi; likes to get together with friends and is a sports lover	**Joy Harry** Teacher at Women's Medical College, Hisar; belongs to Goa; likes to dance and watch films
Sonia Jain Social worker; works for an NGO; lives in Delhi; likes to travel and try new cuisines	**Santosh Kumar** Film director; lives in Pune; likes to exercise and read books

Grammar Guide: Interesting language points

Here are some greetings and expressions we use when we meet people:

Greetings

Hi! I'm .... What's your name?
I don't think we've met before.
I'm ....
What do you do for a living?
What do you do?
Where are you from?
What do you like to do in your free time?
It was nice meeting you. See you later!/I have to leave now. It was nice meeting you. See you!

Responses

Hi ....! I'm ....
Nice to meet you, ...
I'm ....
I am .... What about you?
I am .... What do you do?
I am from ....
Where are you from?
I like to .... and .... What about you?
Nice meeting you, too. Bye!/Same here. Bye!

Saying it right

D1. *Sort*

Listen, repeat and write the words in the correct columns on the basis of their sounds.

Words with the d sound as in *dare*	Words with the th sound as in *there*
____________	____________
____________	____________
____________	____________
____________	____________
____________	____________
____________	____________
____________	____________
____________	____________
____________	____________
____________	____________
____________	____________

D2. *Repeat*

Listen to the words and repeat them. Then, write rhyming words with the sounds ack, all, ank, and ash.

back	small	bank	wash
________	________	________	________
________	________	________	________
________	________	________	________
________	________	________	________
________	________	________	________

Now, read aloud the words that you have written.

Dictation time

E. *Listen and write* — **Listen to the passage and write it in your notebook. Then, take turns to read it out to your partner.**

DT

Communicating and interacting

F. *Interview and introduce* — **Work in pairs and interview your partner. Then, introduce him/her to the class.**

Manners matter!

You should speak politely and in a friendly tone to the interviewee. Give him/her enough time to complete his/her answers. Listen attentively and use positive body language, like nodding, to show that you are getting their point.

Grammar Guide: Interesting language points

Here are some questions that we ask in an interview to know more about our interviewee:

What is your name?
Where were you born?
Where do you live?
How many languages do you know?

What is your favourite food?
What is your favourite film?
What are your good qualities?
What do you want to be when you grow up?

Fun Activity

Creativity • Art Integration NEP

This activity can be played as an entire class. Choose any of the following prompts as the beginning of a story. Then, each of you have to add your own sentence to it. The sentence need not be of the same genre. The next student adds another sentence after what the previous student says to continue the story further. You are allowed to change the genre at your will, as long as your line has a connection to the previous line. This continues till every student has added a line of his or her own.

- The doorbell rang and I opened the front door but to my surprise there was nobody to be seen…
- I wore my new pair of trousers to school today. As I bent down to pick up a coin…
- Just as I was about to sip my tea, I felt a funny sensation in my nose and…

3 Talking about school

In this chapter, we will:

- learn to express our feelings and points of view about something.
- learn to talk about responsibilities in school.
- learn to ask and answer questions.
- learn to talk about things related to school.
- learn to distinguish between similar sounds.

Getting started

Critical Thinking • Communication Skills NEP

A. *Discuss* 3.1

Listen to a radio news clipping talking about the shutdown of schools. Then, discuss the following questions in class.

1. What do you feel about schools being shut down for such reasons?
2. Who gets affected by schools being closed and how do they get affected?
3. Is completing the syllabus in each academic year important? Why/Why not?

Listening and learning

B1. *Choose* 3.2

Listen to a teacher assign classroom duties to her students and choose the correct options.

1. Who is assigned the duty of monitoring classroom discipline?
   a. Shalabh and Smita ☐
   b. Romini and Utkarsh ☐
   c. Disha and Vishesh ☐

2. The teacher has assigned each job to two students. However, one of the jobs has been assigned to only one student. Which job is it?
   a. monitoring the class
   b. taking care of the students' attendance
   c. taking care of the class bulletin board
3. Who is in charge of class cleanliness?
   a. Rohan and Smita
   b. Shalabh and Pakhi
   c. Rohan and Pakhi
4. What responsibility is assigned to Shalabh and Smita?
   a. classroom discipline
   b. the class library
   c. the class bulletin board
5. What is the responsibility given to Disha and Vishesh?
   a. managing the class library
   b. managing class discipline
   c. managing class cleanliness

B2. *Choose* 3.3

Listen to a conversation between Romini and Sonia. Then tick (✓) the things you heard and cross out (✗) the ones you didn't.

1. Some of the students are older than me.
2. I am sure that all of them will listen to me.
3. I am the tallest student in the class.
4. I have such a heavy voice.
5. Don't worry, Romini.
6. Speak to everyone politely but firmly.
7. You should set an example for the class to follow.
8. Your advice is not practical.

Speaking and practising

C1. *Discuss* — **Look at these pictures and then discuss these questions.**

11 SUSTAINABLE CITIES AND COMMUNITIES

1. What do you see in the pictures?
2. What do you think the people in the pictures are doing?
3. What do you think they get in return? Are they doing it for profit?
4. Do you think we can also do something to help those in need? What are the ways through which we can help?
5. Is it important to be kind? Give reasons for your answer.

Grammar Guide: Interesting language points

Here are some introductory phrases we can use to express our views and ideas:

I think...	*My view/opinion is that...*
In my opinion,...	*In my experience...*
It seems to me that...	*As far as I understand/can see...*

C2. *Ask and answer*

Look at the two questionnaires below. Work in pairs. Your partner will ask you the questions in Questionnaire A and you will answer them. Then, you will ask your partner the questions in Questionnaire B and he/she will answer them.

Questionnaire A

	Question	Response
1.	For how long have you been studying in this school?	I have been...
2.	Which subject do you find the most challenging?	The subject that I find...
3.	Which subject do you find the most interesting?	I find...
4.	Are there any new storybooks that you would like to read?	I would like to...
5.	What motivates you to work hard?	...motivates me to work hard.
6.	Who is your ideal person?	My ideal person is...
7.	What is the most important thing about you that everyone should know?	The most important thing about me is...

Questionnaire B

	Question	Response
1.	For how long have you been studying in this school?	I have been...
2.	Which subject do you find the easiest of all?	The subject that I find...
3.	How would you like English to be taught in school?	I would like...
4.	Is there any subject that you find challenging?	I find... challenging.
5.	What do you enjoy doing in your free time?	I enjoy...
6.	What do you think about your town/city/village?	My town/city/village...
7.	What kind of books do you like to read?	I like to read...
8.	What is the most important thing about you that everyone should know?	The most important thing about me is...

Saying it right

D1. *Choose*

3.4

Listen to the words and circle the ones you hear. Then read all the words aloud.

1. boast	both
2. soon	zoom
3. zip	sip
4. fix	fizz
5. lazy	lacy
6. rise	rice
7. peace	peas
8. vast	fast

D2. *Read aloud*

3.5

Read the following sentences aloud. Then, listen to them and check your pronunciation.

1. They both boast a lot.
2. Soon the car went zoom past us.
3. Unzip the bag, take the sipper out and sip to quench your thirst.
4. As soon as we fix the problem, the liquid will start to fizz, don't you think?
5. He is crazily lazy, so he won't make the lacy dress I wanted.
6. The price of rice is on the rise.
7. Let us have peace and not fight over the peas.
8. He ran fast over the vast wasteland.

Dictation time

E. *Listen and write*

DT

Listen to the passage and write it in your notebook. Then, take turns to read it out to your partner.

Interacting and communicating

4 QUALITY EDUCATION

10 REDUCED INEQUALITIES

F1. *Discuss* **It is our responsibility to share knowledge with people who are uneducated. Discuss, as a group, how you can make this possible.**

F2. *Talk* **How can you help your school become a better place? Give suggestions.**

Fun Activity

Talk about classroom rules and discipline with your teacher. Then, draw a poster on it over here.

4 QUALITY EDUCATION

TAKE a break

Which is better?

Here are two pictures.

Picture A

Picture B

One is of homeschooling and the other is of a classroom in a regular school. The word 'homeschooling' is an American term for the practice of teaching one's own children at home, instead of enrolling them to a public or a private school.

Note whatever you see in these two pictures. Then, research on homeschooling, with the help of your parents and the Internet.

Work in pairs. Prepare a short PowerPoint presentation on your research. Present it to your class. One of you may speak on the benefits and problems of regular schooling, while the other talks about the pros and cons of homeschooling.

Neighbourhood Tree Watch

Go around your neighbourhood and spot five different trees. Write their English, vernacular and scientific names. Use the Internet for your research. You may either draw that tree or stick its picture.

Picture of the tree	English name	Vernacular name	Scientific name

4 Our community

In this chapter, we will:

- learn to talk about our community and our responsibilities towards it.
- learn to make plans about doing something for the society.
- learn to express the inability to do something and accept others' refusals.
- learn to say words with th, ill, ink and ing sounds.

Getting started

A. *Discuss* **Use the Internet to find out about a boy named Campbell Remess and his *Project 365*. Discuss these questions after that.**

1. What does Campbell do?
2. Why does he do that?
3. What can you do to contribute towards your community?

Listening and learning

B1. *Gap-fill*

4.1

Swagat Housing Society is organising a health camp for all its residents. Listen to an advertisement about the camp and complete the flyer below.

3 GOOD HEALTH AND WELL-BEING

11 SUSTAINABLE CITIES AND COMMUNITIES

Swagat Housing Society,

in association with ....,

is organising a free ....

for all residents of Swagat Housing Society, Vijay Nagar, Nagpur.

Facilities: Blood sugar test, blood pressure test, ...
.... consultation and .... consultation

Venue: Mahavir Park, opposite ....,

G - Block, Vijay Nagar, Nagpur

Date and time: ...., 9 a.m. – 4 p.m.

Organiser: Swagat Housing Society

Contact: 8006754379

B2. *Choose*

4.2

Listen to an appeal made by the Delhi Traffic Police Commissioner to the people and choose the correct words to fill in the blanks.

Good morning! Welcome to our show City .... (Beat/Heat). I am your host, Varun. Delhi has recently been witnessing a lot of road accidents.

Today, we have with us the Delhi Traffic Police Commissioner, Mr Vinod .... (Bala/Kala), who wants to make an .... (appeal/ apple) to all of you.

Hello everybody, I am Vinod Kala, Commissioner, Delhi Traffic Police. If you were to witness a road accident, there are several things you could do to help those injured.

1. Call the police and the .... (medical/medicine) assistance immediately.
2. Keep the crowd away from the injured so that he/she can stay .... (peaceful/calm) and breathe easily.
3. Stay with the victim till help .... (arrives/leaves).
4. Give the police a .... (sheer/clear) and honest account of the accident, if you witnessed it. This will help the police catch the culprits.

Lend a helping hand and help us keep you safe. Jai Hind!

B3. *True or false* 4.3

Listen to a conversation between two students and mark each statement below as true (T) or false (F).

1. The school is starting a charitable educational programme. ☐
2. The programme will start in the new session. ☐

3. Students from primary or junior classes can volunteer to teach.
4. Each volunteer will get a certificate of appreciation.
5. Free classes for poor children will be held in the morning every day.
6. Leena does not want to volunteer to teach.

Speaking and practising

15 LIFE ON LAND

C1. *Discuss*

Read the following passage about the charitable acts of Aanchal Khanna, a teacher.

Then, work in pairs and think of some acts of charity that you can do to help people and animals in your community. Discuss them with your partner and present your plan to the class.

Aanchal Khanna is a teacher by profession. She is passionate about animals and has been actively involved in ABC (Animal Birth Control) drives in her neighbourhood and adjacent localities.

Stray animals are an important part of her life. She feeds twenty-five dogs every day. She is determined to bring about a change in the mindset of children and has been counselling adults and children about stray animals in their localities.

Aanchal and her team persuade people to adopt Indian breeds of dogs and encourage adoption drives at various places.

Aanchal is doing all she can for the society. What can you do to help your community?

Word Wizard: Useful words and phrases

Here are some introductory phrases we use to express our intentions and plans and to make promises:

I'm going to... I promise... I will...

I will definitely... I plan to...

C2. *Discuss*

Work in small groups. Imagine that there is a charitable organisation collecting money for donating a water tank to a hospital nearby.

3 GOOD HEALTH AND WELL-BEING

How would you help the organisation raise money for the noble cause? Discuss your plan.

Saying it right

D1. *Circle*

4.4

Listen and write the words with the th sound as in *both* and the th sound as in *that*.

Words with th as in *both*	Words with th as in *that*
________	________
________	________
________	________
________	________
________	________

D2. *Repeat and sort*

4.5

Listen and repeat the words with ill, ing and ink endings and write them below.

Words with ill	Words with ing	Words with ink
______	______	______
______	______	______
______	______	______
______	______	______
______	______	______

Dictation time

E. *Listen and write*

DT

Listen to the passage and write it in your notebook. Then, take turns to read it out to your partner.

Interacting and communicating

Critical Thinking NEP

F. *Talk*

Your class is planning a drive to collect old newspapers and give them to some poor people to make bags and earn money.

However, you can't volunteer for this programme for some reason. Think of and give a genuine reason for not being able to participate in the drive. Also, accept others' refusal to volunteer.

Grammar Guide: Interesting language points

Here are some expressions that can be used to express one's inability politely and accept other's refusal nicely:

Expressing inability	Accepting refusal
I wish I could, but...	*It's okay, just make sure...*
Excuse me, ma'am/sir, but...	*All right, but remember...*
I'm sorry, but...	*Oh, that's really sad...*
I really want to participate but...	*No problem/No worries.*

Fun Activity

Critical Thinking NEP

Recently, a 60-year-old woman living alone on Chennai's Anne Besant road was robbed in her home. The police are yet to arrest the culprits. Amid the unsafe situation prevailing in the city for lonely senior citizens, the police have requested them to provide their details so that immediate assistance can be provided when they call for help.

A helpline number has been dedicated to senior citizens' distress calls. Presently, the helpline number receives almost 70 calls per day, with most of the callers requesting for transportation or medical assistance. Work in groups and discuss what else could be done to make senior citizens' lives safer and easier.

5 Shopping on the go

In this chapter, we will:

- learn to have telephonic conversations.
- learn to talk about unpleasant shopping experiences and discuss solutions.
- learn to order food on the phone.
- learn to talk to people and find out about their online shopping preferences.
- learn to say words ending with ock, uck, ump, and unk sounds.
- learn to speak with the right stress and intonation.

Getting started

A. *List*

Make a list of the apps you use to shop online. The list should be in the order of preference. Then, compare your list with your partner's. Which apps do you have in common? Finally, make a list of the apps that are common for the whole class.

Apps you use	Apps your partner uses	Apps common for the whole class

Listening and learning

B1. *Choose* **Listen to a conversation between a customer and a restaurant receptionist and tick (✓) the correct options.**

1. The customer calls the .... food outlet to order food.
   a. My Little Pizza
   b. Little Pizza
2. The customer calls from ....
   a. Sukh Vihar.
   b. Som Vihar.
3. The customer wants to order a ....
   a. medium cheese pizza without any extra topping.
   b. a medium cheese pizza with a topping of olives, extra cheese and mushrooms.

4. The total amount that the customer has to pay is ....
   a. ₹ 540.
   b. ₹ 514.
5. The customer wants to pay ....
   a. cash.
   b. by debit card.
6. The customer also orders ....
   a. garlic bread and a bottle of juice.
   b. garlic Supreme bread and a bottle of cola.

B2. *True or false* 5.2

Listen to a conversation between a customer and a customer support executive and mark each statement as true (T) or false (F).

a. The customer calls the Paradise Television company. ☐

b. She calls to complain about her 36-inch LED TV. ☐

c. She complains of the poor quality of the television sound. ☐

d. The television was bought on 25th January 2017. ☐

e. The woman doesn't have the bill of purchase with her. ☐

f. The customer support executive assures the customer of an engineer's visit in 48 hours. ☐

g. The customer lives at Civil Lines, Chandigarh. ☐

Speaking and practising

Experiential Learning • Collaboration NEP

C1. *Role-play*

Work in pairs. Call up your favourite restaurant and place an order. Your partner will play the role of the restaurant receptionist and take your order. Make sure you include necessary details like your name, address, the things you have ordered, and your mode of payment. Choose the food items from this menu.

Spicy Food

MENU

Starters and salads

Tomato soup	₹ 80
Mushroom soup	₹ 100
Sweetcorn soup	₹ 100
Green salad	₹ 60
Russian salad	₹ 90
Peanut crunch salad	₹ 110

Drinks

Mineral water	₹ 25
Fresh fruit juice (seasonal)	₹ 35
Tea	₹ 15
Coffee	₹ 20

Main Course

Pasta in red sauce with garlic bread	₹ 200
The all-cheese pasta with garlic bread	₹ 200
Red/Green Thai curry with steamed rice	₹ 250
Noodles with dry Manchurian	₹ 250
Vegetable rolls (potato/paneer/soya)	₹ 200

Desserts

Fruit salad and ice cream	₹ 150
Ice cream (coffee/strawberry/ chocolate) (single scoop)	₹ 50
Lemon cake (one slice)	₹ 80
Cheese cake (one slice)	₹ 100
Chocolate cake (one slice)	₹ 80

Grammar Guide: Interesting language points

Here are some useful expressions you can use:

Customer

I would like...
Could you please...?
Yes, please...
How long will that...?
Thank you.

Restaurant receptionist

May I take your order, please?
Would you like...?
Anything else?
Please give me your...
Have a great day!

C2. *Discuss* **Read the following problems that we often face while we shop or use any online services. Form groups and discuss various possible solutions to the problems.**

1. You book a taxi online and travel to a busy market. You leave the taxi and go to the market. After half an hour, you realise that you left one of your bags containing important papers in the cab. What would you do?
2. You purchased a pair of jeans online using a popular shopping app. The jeans do not fit you and you return them. You expect that the whole amount of the purchase will be refunded to you soon. However, the company does not make the refund to you because the return does not get recorded in their system. What would you do?
3. You order a pair of branded headphones online. When you receive the item, you see that it's not original, but a fake product. What would you do?
4. Your mother orders groceries online, but the fruits and vegetables delivered are not fresh at all. What would you suggest to your mother?

Word Wizard: Useful words and phrases

Here are some words, phrases and expressions you can include in your discussion:

important certificates	too tight	poor quality
exchange	refund	stale and rotten
I suggest...	First of all....	I could...
It's always better to...	I will...	It might be a good idea...

Saying it right

D1. *Repeat* 5.3

Listen and repeat the words paying special attention to the f sound.

fur	fingers	fire	fudge
food	fish	four	fork

D2. *Repeat and write* 5.4

Listen to some words with ock, uck, ump and unk sounds and repeat and write them.

Words with ock	Words with uck	Words with ump	Words with unk
______	______	______	______
______	______	______	______
______	______	______	______
______	______	______	______
______	______	______	______
______	______	______	______

D3. *Read aloud* 5.5

Read the following sentences aloud with the right intonation. Then, listen to these sentences and repeat them.

1. I'm so busy these days that I seldom get a chance to catch up with my friends.
2. I get on really well with my friend but I just can't stand his brother.
3. I don't earn a lot but I make enough to get by.
4. I can't stand dirt, grime or filth.
5. There's no way I am going to the party if you aren't coming.

Dictation time

E. *Listen and write* DT

Listen to the passage and write it in your notebook. Then, take turns to read it out to your partner.

Interacting and communicating

F. *Conduct a survey* — **Look at the survey sheet below. Conduct a survey of six persons and present your conclusions to the class.**

Questions to ask	Student 1	Student 2	Student 3	Student 4	Student 5	Student 6
1. Which app do you use most often to buy books online?						
2. Which app do you use most often to buy clothes online?						
3. Which app do you use most often to buy groceries online?						
4. Which app do you use most often to buy electronics online?						
5. Which app do you use most often to download songs?						
6. Which app do you use most often to book a cab?						

Fun Activity

Work in pairs and perform this activity in front of the entire class.

Imagine that you are at the market. One of you plays the role of a person who needs to buy a home appliance. Your partner should play the shopkeeper.

You must describe the product through mime instead of actually saying it out loud. Your partner must be able to correctly guess the appliance you are asking for by looking at your gesture and write the answer on the board. Neither of you must utter a word.

Take turns to play both the roles.

6 At the bank

In this chapter, we will:

- learn to talk about banking.
- learn to make complaints.
- learn to make plans for a party.
- learn to say words with the th, ee and oo sounds.

Getting started

A. *Answer*

Look at these pictures. They show the different services of a bank. Then, answer the questions.

1. What services do we get at the bank?
2. Who are the people shown in the picture?
3. What are the three people in the top left picture doing?

Listening and learning

Cross-curricular NEP

B1. *Identify* 6.1

Mr Sharma wants to open a savings account in a bank. He visits the bank to get necessary information. Listen to his conversation with the customer support executive and identify which documents are required. Tick (✓) the documents that are required and cross out (✗) the documents that are not required.

1. A copy of the passport/ration card ☐
2. A copy of the Aadhar card ☐
3. A copy of the medical fitness certificate ☐
4. A copy of the bank statement for the last three months ☐
5. A copy of an electricity bill /a water bill ☐
6. A copy of a property tax receipt ☐
7. A copy of the marriage certificate ☐
8. A copy of the character certificate ☐
9. A copy of the PAN card ☐
10. A copy of the Post Office savings account statement ☐

Digital Literacy • Cross-curricular NEP

B2. *Gap-fill* 6.2

Listen to a description of mobile banking and fill in the blanks.

1. Mobile banking is usually .... round the clock.
2. Mobile banking enables us to make .... without visiting the bank.
3. We can .... money to others' bank accounts using mobile banking.
4. Mobile banking is faster and more convenient than .... banking.

5. It saves us the time and effort needed to .... the bank physically.

6. Mobile banking does away with the expenses needed to withdraw, ... and transfer cash.

Speaking and practising

Cross-curricular NEP

C1. *Role-play and write*

Work in pairs. Role-play a conversation between a bank customer and a bank assistant. Fill in the necessary details in the bank deposit slip and seek the bank assistant's help to deposit your money.

इंडिया बैंक India Bank

दिनांक Date ☐☐☐

______________ शाखा Branch

बचत बैंक / संचयी जमा खाता सं.
Saving Bank / Cumulative Deposite A/C No.

☐☐☐☐☐☐☐☐☐☐☐☐☐☐☐

के नाम जमा / of ______________

नकदी/चेक Details of Cash/Cheque	राशि Amount रू. Rs.	 पै. P.
रू. शब्दों में Rs. in Words ______		

बुक Book - 2337 - (20 Lvs.)
Edn Stores - 3 Lacs Books/4-2010 खजांची Cashier

इंडिया बैंक India Bank

दिनांक Date ☐☐☐

______________ शाखा Branch

के नाम जमा हेतु FOR THE CRIDIT OF ______________

बचत बैंक / संचयी जमा खाता सं.
Saving Bank / Cumulative Deposite A/C No.

☐☐☐☐☐☐☐☐☐☐☐☐☐☐☐

जिस बैंक पर आहरित Drawn on Bank	शाखा Branch	चेक नं. Cheque No.	चेक नोट Cash Notes	राशि Amount रू. Rs.			 पै. P.
			× 1000				
			× 500				
			× 100				
			× 50				
			× 20				
			× 10				
रू. शब्दों में Rs. in Words ______			सिक्के Coins				
खजांची Cashier	स्क्रोल Scroll	अधिकारी Officer	योग Total				
				जमाकर्ता (हस्ताक्षर) Deposited by (Signature)			

कृपया नगद जमा, इस बैंक पर आहरित लिखतों, समाशोधन लिखतों और बहारी केन्द्र के लिखतों के लिए अलग अलग स्लिप का प्रयोग करें।
Use separate slips of depositing cash, instruments drawn on this Bank, clearing instruments & outstation instruments.
प्रिय ग्राहक, आपकी बेहतर सेवा हेतु कृपया हमें सहयोग करें, कृपया जमा पर्ची अपना पता पूर्व सम्पर्क ब्यौरा अघतन करें।
Dear Customer, Please help us in serving you better. Kindly update your address and contact details on the reverse of this paying-in-slip.

Word Wizard: Interesting language points

Here are some expressions that you can use in the role-play:

Customer	**Bank assistant**
What shall I write here?	How may I help?
What is to be written here?	This is where you write your ....
Is this where I write ....?	Yes, fill in your .... here.
What shall I do after filling up the slip?	After you've filled up the slip, please take the slip and the money to the cash deposit counter.

C2. *Discuss*

Suppose you want to surprise your mother on her birthday by giving her a gift. How will you save money for buying it and what gift will you buy for her?

Work with a partner and discuss it with him/her. Then, discuss it as a class to know about their ideas on saving money and buying the gift.

Grammar Guide: Interesting language points

You can include these phrases in your discussion:

I will buy...

I am going to...

The best possible things would be to...

I will probably...

I think I will...

What will you...

Saying it right

D1. *Gap-fill* 6.3

Listen to the sentences and fill in each blank with the correct word from the box.

thinker	thick	thin	thing	think	there

1. The child has a .... book in his hands.
2. .... are a few shops in the lane.
3. What is that .... over there?
4. My sister is very ....
5. I must .... of an idea.
6. He was a great ....

D2. *Repeat and write*

Listen, repeat and write the words with *ee* and *oo* sounds in the correct columns.

Words with the *ee* sound	Words with the *oo* sound
________________	________________
________________	________________
________________	________________
________________	________________
________________	________________
________________	________________
________________	________________
________________	________________

D3. *Practise*

Work with a partner and practise the following conversation.

A: Can you tell me about a typical day in your life?

B: Yes, um... I get up early in the morning because it gives me enough time to get ready.

A: Hmm...

B: You know, usually after 8, the traffic starts to become heavier, so I start off before that.

A: Okay. How far is your school?

B: My school is only four or five kilometers from where I live, but it takes me more than half an hour to reach there if the traffic is heavy.

A: Do you go by bus?

B: Usually, my dad drops me but sometimes I cycle there. I use my bike that I got on my birthday last year.

A: Okay.

Now carry on the conversation on your own with your partner.

Dictation time

E. *Listen and write*

Listen to the passage and write it in your notebook. Then, take turns to read it out to your partner.

Interacting and communicating

Communication Skills NEP

F1. *Role-play*

Listen to a customer complain about a problem to a bank employee. Pay attention to the speakers' tones. Then, work in pairs and practise the dialogue.

Bank employee:	Hello! How may I help you?
Customer:	I have a complaint about my ATM card. I received my new debit card a week ago but the password does not work.
Bank employee:	Please, have a seat. Let me have a look at the card... I am sorry, sir, but your card has been blocked by the bank.
Customer:	Blocked! But why? I've been trying to use the card for the past one week and it keeps showing the error message 'transaction failed'!
Bank employee:	I'm sorry for the inconvenience, sir. The card was blocked because a wrong password was typed in more than three times. But don't worry; it will take only two days to get your card activated again.
Customer:	Okay, the print of the password was so bad that I couldn't read it properly. Please issue me a new password.
Bank employee:	Yes, I'm registering your request for that. Your password will be sent to you within two days.
Customer:	Thank you very much.

Creativity NEP

F2. *Complain* — **Work in pairs. Role-play a conversation between a bank employee and a customer. Take turns and complain about a banking problem.**

Word Wizard: Useful words and phrases

Here are some words and phrases you can include in your complaint:

ATM	command	withdrawal alert
amount deducted	savings account	no cash dispensed
no information on enquiry		

Fun Activity

Critical Thinking • Cross-curricular NEP

Can you earn and think of saving some money?

If you were to earn ₹ 500 in a week, how would you do that? Think of some practical ways of earning and saving money. Share them with your class.

TAKE a break

Cheque your money

Do you know what is a cheque? Have you seen one at home or at the bank? Look carefully at the image of a cheque given below.

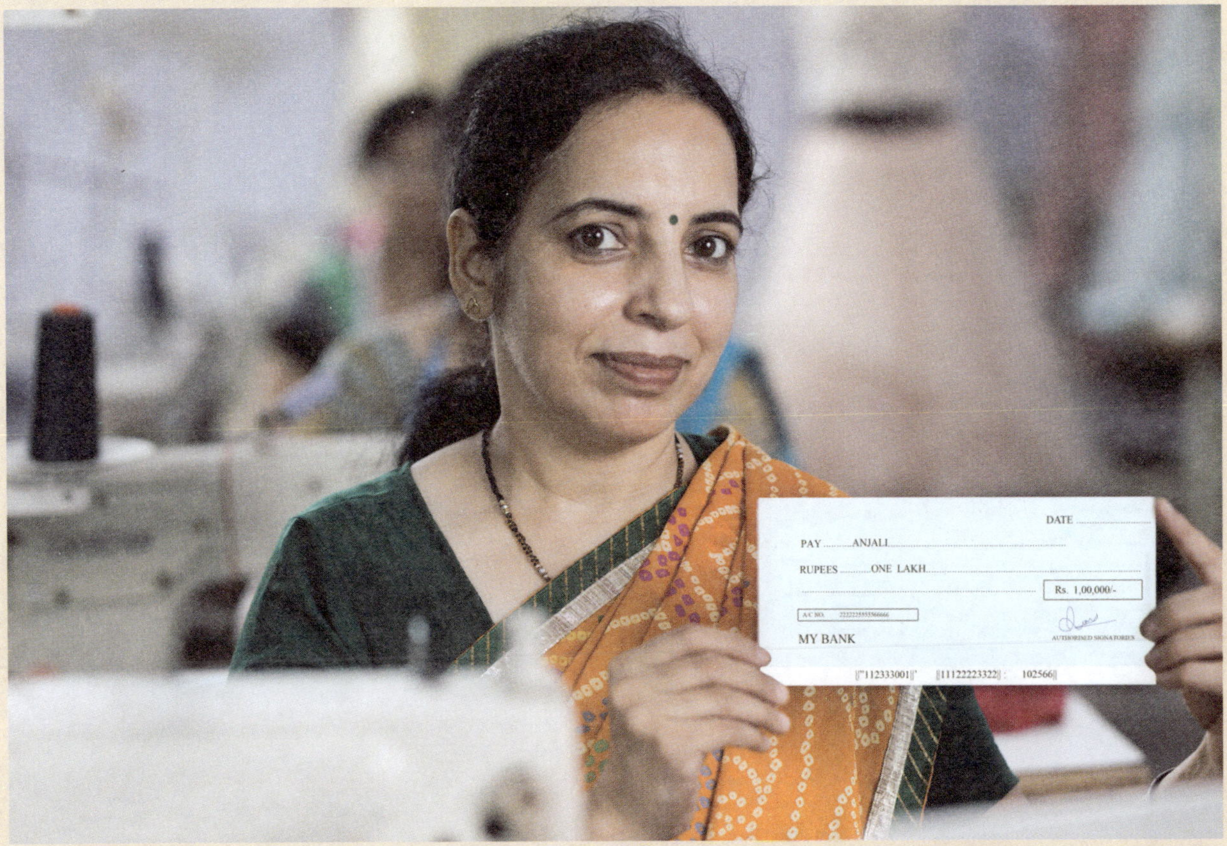

A cheque is a document used to deposit money in an account or transfer money from one account to another. It is a convenient way of doing transactions without using cash.

At home, ask your parents for a cancelled cheque. Paste it here and with their help, label its different parts.

7 My dreams

In this chapter, we will:

- learn to talk about our dreams and ambitions.
- learn to listen and extract necessary information.
- learn to ask people about their aspirations and goals and tell them ours.
- learn to say sentences with correct pauses and mark the pauses in writing.

Getting started

A. *Read*

Read the following passage about the young Indian golfer Aditi Ashok.

Aditi Ashok was born on 29th March 1998 in Bangalore. She started playing golf at the age of five. She is now a professional golf player who also took part in the 2016 Summer Olympics. She is the first and youngest Indian to win the Lalla Aicha Tour School. With that victory, she secured her Ladies European Tour card for the 2016 season. Ashok is the only Indian golfer who has played the Asian Youth Games (2013), the Youth Olympic Games (2014), the Asian Games (2014) and the Olympic Games (2016).

She is the winner of the 2016 Hero Women's Indian Open and the first Indian to win a Ladies European Tour title.

Ashok has achieved a lot at a very young age and has made her country proud of her.

What do you wish to do in your life? Tell your ambitions to the class.

Listening and learning

B1. *Match* 7.1

Listen to the definitions of the following professions and match the sentence parts correctly.

1. An aviator
2. A statistician
3. A disc jockey
4. A meteorologist
5. A paediatrician
6. An ornithologist
7. A comptroller
8. A radiologist

a. introduces and plays recorded popular music.

b. studies the Earth's atmosphere and its changes.

c. looks after the financial accounts of a business company.

d. is a doctor who treats children's diseases.

e. studies birds.

f. flies an aircraft.

g. studies and uses different types of radiation to treat diseases.

h. studies and analyses information that is in the form of numbers.

B2. *Gap-fill* 7.2

Listen to the poem *I Wish* and fill in the missing words.

I Wish

I wish I may, I wish I ....,
For something good to come in sight.
I wish to see my .... star,
And maybe it will come tonight.

And with that star I plan to wish,
For all I love to come to me.
My .... and dreams I will soon see,
All that's needed is to wish for thee.

This is how I used to think,
Before I realized wishing is like a ....
When you wink you hope to show,
But never really are able to know.

Wishing won't make your dreams come true,
That is only something .... can do.
If you want something to happen,
It's .... who'll have to do the snapping.

So if you're going to make a wish,
On a .... a star will fish.
Make a wish for .... and ....,
At least this will be something to ....

Wishing is all fine and dandy,
As long as you don't make it handy.
Wishing is for you to ....,
If you want success, you're better to scheme.

Speaking and practising

Collaboration NEP

C1. *Ask and answer*

Recite the poem in the listening task B2. Then, ask and answer the following questions in groups of five.

1. What message does the poet give in the poem?
2. What/Who do you think is the *shining star*?
3. Why does the poet say that wishing is like winking?
4. Who does the poet say will make your dreams come true?
5. What does the poet say one should wish for, if one wishes for anything at all?

Collaboration • Critical Thinking NEP

C2. *Ask and answer*

Work in pairs. Take turns to ask and answer the following questions.

1. What is your main goal in life?
2. How do you plan to achieve that goal?
3. What are your goals in school?
4. Who is your role model? Why?
5. What would you like to be doing in 30 years' time?
6. What do you think the world will be like in 2050?
7. How important is it to have hopes and ambitions? Discuss.

Grammar Guide: Interesting language points

You can begin your responses as follows:

My main goal in life is...
I will/I am determined to...
My goal in school is...
My role model is...
I hope I will be...
I think...
I believe it is...

Saying it right

D. *Repeat and punctuate*

7.3

Listen to the sentences and repeat them. Also, insert a comma or a semicolon appropriately to mark the pause in each sentence.

1. Leena I really like your paintings.
2. You don't need to worry about the tickets I'll book them.
3. Sorry I didn't get your point.
4. I would like to watch a Hollywood film Bollywood films are too long.
5. I am planning to settle in a village I am fed up with the city life.
6. I need a notebook a black pen and a pencil.
7. Lucknow is the capital of Uttar Pradesh the most populous state of India.
8. My most favourite poet is Rabindranath Tagore the first Asian to win the Nobel Prize.

Info byte

A comma in writing indicates a short pause. A semicolon indicates a pause longer than a comma but shorter than a full stop. A semicolon is often used to join two sentences that are closely related. For example, 'Sorry I can't watch the film today; I have to prepare for my exams.'

Dictation time

E. *Listen and write*

DT

Listen to the passage and write it in your notebook. Then, take turns to read it out to your partner.

Interacting and communicating

Creativity NEP

F. *Deliver a speech*

Imagine that you have become a very famous personality, such as a film star, an artist, an astronaut or a politician.

Make a two-minute speech about your success and rise to fame and how you wish to contribute towards society. Write and rehearse your speech before you deliver it in class.

Manners matter!

Be confident and focus on giving your message as clearly as possible. Expressions like cheerfulness and seriousness should be visible on your face in accordance with the content of your speech. Maintain an eye contact with the audience. Be loud enough for everybody to hear you well.

Don't forget to address your audience respectfully in the beginning.

Fun Activity

Experiential Learning NEP

Talk to your parents and grandparents about what they wished to be in life when they were your age. Could they make life decisions on their own, or did their parents decide for them? Have they achieved their goals in life? Have they fulfilled their dreams and ambitions? What do they wish for you? Share the summary of your conversations with the class.

8 Let's party

In this chapter, we will:

- learn to invite, accept and refuse invitations.
- learn to offer food and beverages to guests.
- learn to accept or refuse offers of food or beverage politely.
- learn to compliment people and accept compliments with gratitude.
- learn to say words with the soft c and the hard c sounds.

Getting started

Communication Skills • Collaboration NEP

A. *Invite*

Look at the pictures. Work in pairs and invite your partner to these events. Your partner will accept or refuse the invitations politely.

Example:

Priya: Hi, Pradeep. I am holding my birthday party on 15th April at my house. Please do come to my party.

Pradeep: Sure, Priya. Thanks for the invitation.

Listening and learning

B1. *Gap-fill*

8.1

Listen to these conversations and fill in the blanks.

1. Nitya: I think I ate too much.
   Ria: Why don't we ....?
2. Reema: My room is so messy!
   Shreya: Let's ....
3. Karan: I am very hungry.
   Kishor: Let's ....
4. Shilpa: It's so nice and sunny today.
   Pia: How about ....?
5. Shloka: I'm feeling so sleepy.
   Rahul: Why don't you ....? You'll feel better.
6. Ashok: This place is so scary.
   Asha: ....
7. Manish: It's so hot in Alwar!
   Gunjan: Why ....?
8. Tom: Papa has installed a new video game in the computer.
   Pankaj: .... tonight.

B2. Choose

8.2

Listen to these conversations. In each of them, an invitation is either being accepted or refused. Listen carefully and choose the correct option.

1.	Accepted	☐	Refused	☐
2.	Accepted	☐	Refused	☐
3.	Accepted	☐	Refused	☐
4.	Accepted	☐	Refused	☐
5.	Accepted	☐	Refused	☐
6.	Accepted	☐	Refused	☐
7.	Accepted	☐	Refused	☐

Speaking and practising

Collaboration NEP

C1. *Invite and respond*

Work in pairs. Take turns and invite your partner to the given events. Your partner may accept or refuse the invitations.

Give necessary details when you invite him/her. If you refuse an invitation, do that politely, giving a suitable reason for your refusal.

1. Lunch at your house
2. Birthday party at your house
3. Tennis match in your local sports complex
4. Family picnic
5. School fete

Grammar Guide: Interesting language points

Here are some expressions that can be used to invite others, accept invitations and refuse invitations:

Invite	Accept	Refuse
I'm throwing a party at my house this evening to celebrate...	*Sure. Thanks for the invitation.*	*Sorry, I have an appointment with the dentist this evening.*
Do you want to go to...?	*Sure. What time?*	*Sorry, I can't. I have some urgent work to do.*
Would you like...?	*I'd love to, thanks.*	*Sorry, I'm very busy tomorrow.*
Would you be interested in...?	*That's very kind of you, thanks.*	*That's very kind of you, but...*
How about going to...?	*That sounds lovely. Thank you.*	*Well, I'd love to, but...*
I'm throwing a... party tomorrow at... Please do attend.	*What a great idea! Thank you.*	*I'm really sorry, but...*
	Sure. When should I be there?	*Sorry, I don't think I can as...*

C2. *Enact*

8.3

Ashmit has invited his friends to dinner. Listen to the conversation Ashmit has with his friends.

Ashmit: Thank you all for coming tonight to the dinner. It's great to see you all after such a long time.

Siya: Yes, it's wonderful to meet everyone. Thanks for the invitation.

Ashmit: You are welcome, Siya. So, what would you like to drink: juice, soft drink or lemonade?

Rukmini: I'd like to have some orange juice, please.

Ashmit: What about you, Siya and Karan? What would you like?

Siya: No thanks, I don't need anything to drink.

Karan: Neither do I. I'm fine.

Ashmit: Let's have dinner then. Would anyone like chapattis with rice?

Karan: Yes, I'll take one chapatti.

Rukmini: I'll only have rice with curry.

Ashmit: Have some French fries, Karan.

Karan: Sorry, I don't think I will. I'm avoiding fried food these days.

Ashmit: What about you, Siya? Would you like some more fries?

Siya: Yes, I'd love some more, thanks. They are really yummy.

Ashmit: We have butter chicken too. Would anyone like some?

Rukmini: Yes, I'd like that.

Karan: No, thanks. I'm a vegetarian. I'll just have the vegetables and dal.

Now, work in groups of five and enact the situation in the class. Take turns inviting your friends for the party and accepting the invitation. Remember, the host will offer food and soft drinks to all his guests. The friends will accept or refuse the food offer politely as per their liking.

Saying it right

D1. *Repeat and classify*

8.4

Listen to these words with the hard c sound as in *cap* and words with the soft c sound as in *city*. Repeat the words and write them in the correct column.

Hard c words	Soft c words
______________________	______________________
______________________	______________________
______________________	______________________
______________________	______________________
______________________	______________________
______________________	______________________

D2. *Punctuate*

8.5

Listen to this recipe. As you listen, punctuate the passage appropriately by inserting commas and semicolons to mark pauses.

Lemonade is a refreshing drink it quenches our thirst and hydrates our body. We all like to drink cool lemonade especially in summer. Here is a recipe to make a lemonade.

Cut 4–5 lemons in half. Squeeze the lemon pieces with a lemon-squeezer and collect the juice in a jug. Add a glass of water to the juice. Next add two or three spoons of sugar according to your taste.

Stir the solution well with a spoon. When the sugar is fully dissolved your lemonade is ready. Keep the lemonade in the refrigerator for a few minutes for cooling cool lemonade tastes better. Alternately you can also add ice cubes to cool it quickly. Enjoy the cool lemonade!

Dictation time

E. *Listen and write*

DT

Listen to the passage and write it in your notebook. Then, take turns to read it out to your partner.

Interacting and communicating

F. *Compliment*

Work in pairs and choose five classmates you would like to compliment. You can compliment them on their hairstyle, intelligence, smartness, for something they cooked, etc. Choose five different criteria to compliment.

First, write the compliments against their names. And then, give them the compliments.

- Name: ____________________
- Compliments: ____________________
- Name: ____________________
- Compliments: ____________________
- Name: ____________________
- Compliments: ____________________
- Name: ____________________
- Compliments: ____________________
- Name: ____________________
- Compliments: ____________________

Word Wizard: Useful words and phrases

Here are some expressions you can use to compliment people and accept compliments from them:

Appearance

You look smart today.

I like your new hairstyle.

This hairstyle really suits you.

Work

You worked very hard on this.

You've done a great job!

Good job!

This is excellent.

Talent

You're a great artist.

You have a lovely voice.

You dance really well!

Food

You make very tasty sandwiches.

I loved the pasta you made.

You are a great cook.

Accepting compliments

Thank you.

Thank you for your kind words.

I really appreciate that.

You're so kind.

It's really kind of you to say that.

Thank you so much.

Fun Activity

Creativity NEP

You have performed exceptionally well in your annual exams this year and your parents have invited your friends for a lunch party to celebrate your success. Prepare an invitation card for your friends.

The invitation must include the details of the occasion, time, place as well as contact details.

9 Entertainment

In this chapter, we will:

- learn to express our opinions about films and TV shows.
- learn to answer questions on the basis of listening.
- learn to book tickets over the telephone.
- learn to distinguish between the different i sounds, and the soft and hard g sounds.

Getting started

Communication Skills NEP

A. *Discuss*

Have you watched a film or read an interesting book recently? Work with a partner and discuss what you liked or disliked about the film/book. You can talk about the following points.

1. What is the main idea of the film/book?
2. Who is your most favourite character and why?
3. Would you recommend this film/book to others? Why/Why not?

Listening and learning

B1. *Choose*

Listen to a conversation between Ravi and Rohit and choose the correct options.

1. Rohit wants to watch the film
   a. *Superman.* ☐
   b. *Batman.* ☐
   c. *The Jungle Book.* ☐

2. The main character in the story is
   a. Mowgli.
   b. Winnie the Pooh.
   c. Peter Pan.
3. It is based on the work of
   a. J. K. Rowling.
   b. Lewis Carroll.
   c. Rudyard Kipling.
4. The film has been nominated for the
   a. Academy Awards.
   b. Golden Globe Awards.
   c. American Academy Awards.
5. Rohit and Ravi decide to watch the show that starts at
   a. 3 p.m.
   b. 4 p.m.
   c. 6 p.m.
6. The film is showing at
   a. Grand Cinema.
   b. Regal Cinema.
   c. Royal Cinema.

B2. *Gap-fill*

9.2

Listen to a conversation between Navit and Rohit and fill in the blanks.

Navit: Hi, Rohit! How are you?

Rohit: Hi, Navit! I'm fine. How about you?

Navit: I'm fine too. How was your ....?

Rohit: It was very .... I spent most of the day reading *The Jungle Book* by Rudyard Kipling. Then, I watched the film .... on the book.

Navit: I see. How did you like the book?

Rohit: It's a very interesting story of a boy named Mowgli, who is raised by a pack of .... in the jungle. It's really gripping.

Navit: Great. And how about the film?

Rohit: I enjoyed the film too. Though it was released in ...., I had not watched it before. I loved the .... of the boy who played Mowgli.

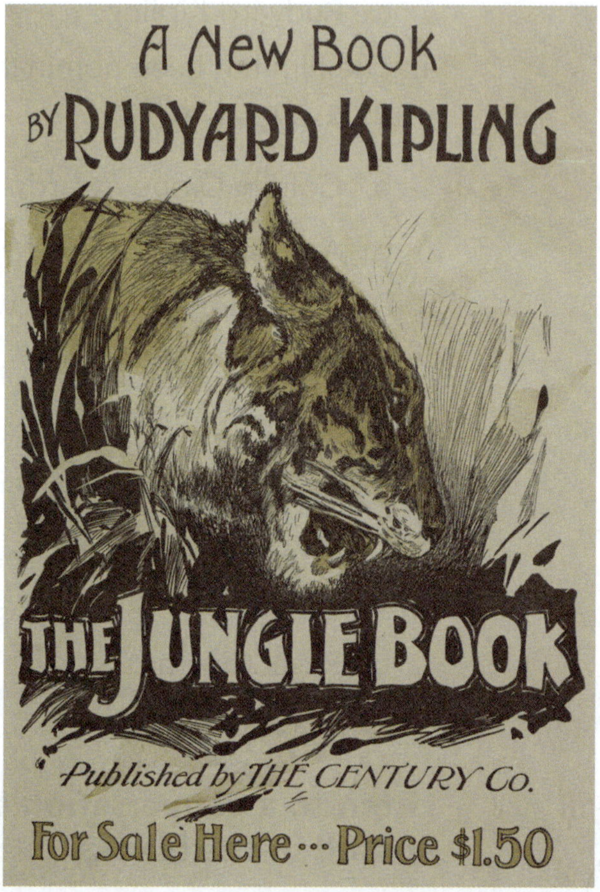

Navit: I see. Do you know who played the .... of Mowgli in the film?

Rohit: Yes, a boy named Neel Sethi played the role. Neel lives in New York. His .... moved to the US from India many years ago.

Navit: Ok, I will read the book .... and watch the film too.

Speaking and practising

Communication Skills NEP

C1. *Discuss* **Read this conversation between two friends.**

Gauri: Hi, Rama. Did you watch *The Wizard of Oz* last night?

Rama: No, I couldn't. I was watching my favourite show *The Nancy Drew Mysteries*. I love the show and didn't want to miss it. How was the film?

Gauri: It was fantastic. You must watch it when you get a chance.

Rama: I surely will.

Now, work in groups of three and discuss your favourite film or TV programme.

Word Wizard: Useful words and phrases

Here are some introductory phrases used to express likes and dislikes:

Expressing likes	Expressing dislikes
I like...	I don't like...
I love...	I dislike...
I adore...	I hate...
I'm crazy about...	I can't tolerate...
I'm mad about...	I can't bear...
I enjoy...	I can't stand...

Communication Skills NEP

C2. *Talk* **Form groups of four and talk about a TV show or a film that you all have seen. Express your views about it. You may agree or disagree with others' opinions.**

Word Wizard: Useful words and phrases

You can use the following expressions to express your opinion, or to agree or disagree with someone:

Expressing opinion	Agreeing with an opinion	Disagreeing with an opinion
I think...	I agree with this...	I'm afraid, I don't agree with you.
It seems to me that...	I completely agree with this view...	Sorry, I disagree with you.
In my opinion...	This is absolutely right.	Sorry, but I don't agree with you.
From my point of view...	You're right, but...	Sorry, but I have to differ with you.
As far as I understand...	I agree with you, but...	
As far as I see...		

Saying it right

D1. *Identify* 9.3

Listen and circle the words with the i sound as in *kit*. Underline the words with the i sound as in *sheep* and tick (✓) the words with the i sound as in *happy*.

lid	lead	lite	rally
did	deed	fill	feel
fit	feet	actually	grin
green	factually	hit	heat
is	ease	smartly	meet
slip	sleep	still	steal

D2. *Repeat and write*

Listen, repeat and write the words in the correct columns on the basis of the soft g sound as in *gym* and and hard g sound as in *gas*.

Soft g words	Hard g words
________	________
________	________
________	________
________	________
________	________
________	________
________	________
________	________

Dictation time

E. *Listen and write*

Listen to the passage and write it in your notebook. Then, take turns to read it out to your partner.

Interacting and communicating

Communication Skills • Collaboration NEP

F. *Gap-fill*

Listen to a girl booking tickets for a film and fill in the ticket details.

.... Cinema

Name of the movie: ....

Seat numbers: .... and ....

(....................... section)

Show timings: ....

Price of the tickets: ₹......................

Total amount including taxes: ₹...................

Now, work with a partner and have a similar conversation.

Fun Activity

Cross-curricular NEP

Sport is now as much virtual as it is physical. Games can now be played on multiple platforms, like smartphones, Xbox, PC, etc., as long as you have a stable Internet connection.

Now, choose a virtual game that you like and brainstorm on the following questions. If you do not currently like any virtual games, think of a game that you would have liked if it were made according to your taste of games.

- What is the name of the game and in which platforms can it be played?
- Does the game has a unique or fantastic name? If so, then what is the reason behind it?
- Is it for a certain age group or can it be played across all ages?
- Do you think gaming has any negative impacts? What can they be? How should you deal with them?
- What are the USPs of the game you like? Does it have any positive impact too? If so, what are they?

At the end of your brainstorming, make an advertisement poster for your game, and present it to your class.

TAKE a break

Public Speaking

Have you ever seen a performance by a stand-up comedian? Or a film in which the actor captivates you with their dialogue? Or even an important public speaker who captures your attention when he/she speaks? What is common between all of them?

Speaking in public or to an audience is a skilful craft. It requires the speaker to keep a few important things in mind as shown below.

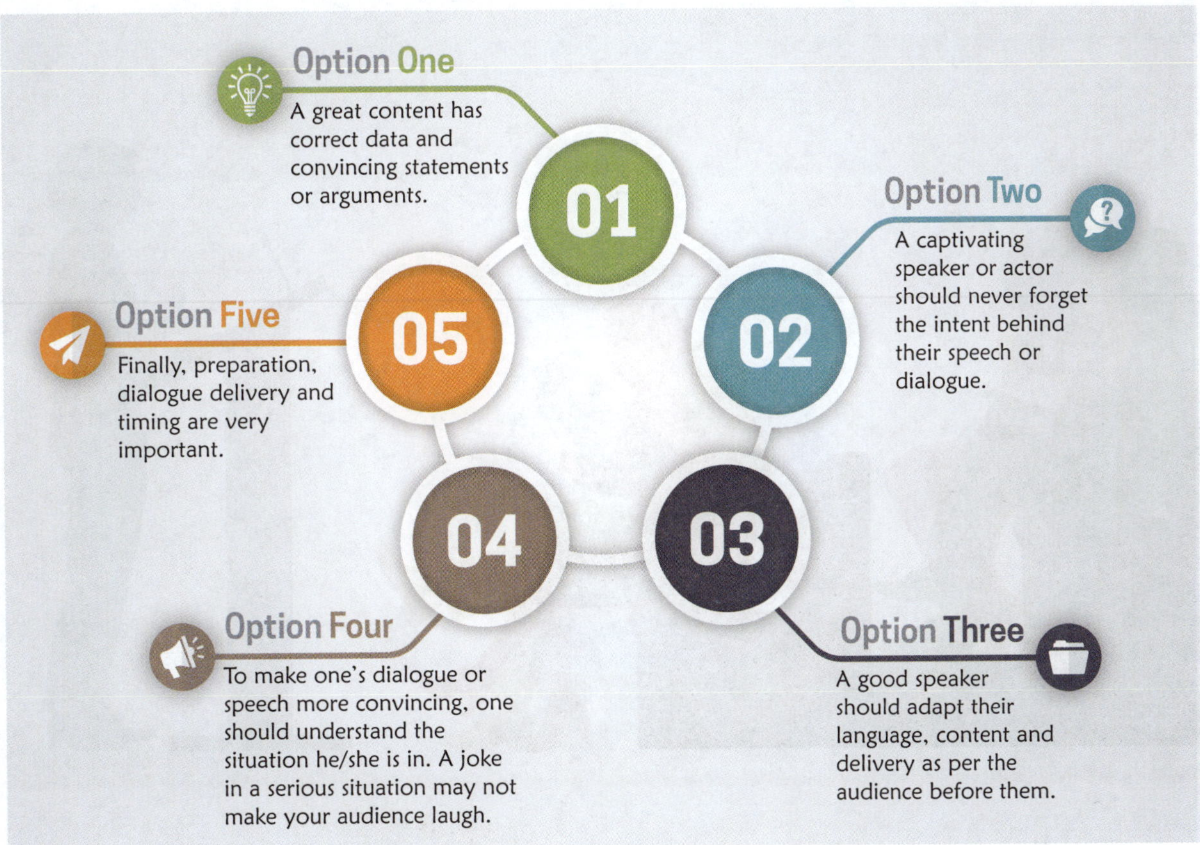

Now, prepare a short speech of about one minute on any one of the following topics and then present it to your class. You may use flash cards or keep your written speech with you, so that you can refer to it.

1. It's your friend's birthday and you have prepared a toast.
2. You are talking to your RWA Secretary about keeping your neighbourhood dust-free.
3. You are trying to convince your grandparents about establishing colonies in Mars.
4. You are a budding stand-up comedian or an actor, and you have to interact with your audience or present a captivating dialogue.
5. You are convincing your teacher that handicrafts like carpentry, sewing, etc. are necessary skills and should be taught in schools.

10 Getting our point across

In this chapter, we will:

- learn to give and follow directions.
- learn to complete dialogues.
- learn to interrupt people politely and to respond to others.
- learn to disagree with others politely.
- learn to say words with the sound of a as in *cap* and a as in *bath*.

Getting started

Collaboration • Critical Thinking NEP

A. *Give directions*

Working in pairs, give your friend directions to your house from the school. Be clear and mention important landmarks so that your friend is able to find and reach your house easily.

Critical Thinking NEP

B1. *Map reading* 10.1

Look at the map given here. Listen to some people giving directions to certain places on the map. Can you identify the places?

B2. *Gap-fill* 10.2

Listen to the directions again and complete the sentences with the correct words.

1. It's the building next to the museum, on the ....
2. After driving for a few minutes, you will reach a ....

3. Just after the roundabout, you will see a ....
....

4. Take the first .... turn onto Back Street. It's the building next to the museum.

B3. *Gap-fill*

10.3

Listen to a class in progress. The teacher is teaching Class VII the history of the Mughal rule in India. Listen carefully and complete the sentences.

1. Rohit says '...' when he interrupts the teacher to tell her what his father says.
2. The teacher asks Rohit to let her finish first and resumes teaching by saying, 'Now, ... ?'
3. Koel says, '...' before asking her question.
4. The teacher resumes teaching by saying, 'To get ....'
5. Saba interrupts the teacher and asks whether the Taj Mahal was built ....
6. The teacher resumes teaching by saying, 'Now, ... ?'

Speaking and practising

Critical Thinking NEP

C1. *Give directions*

Work in pairs and ask your partner for directions to a place in the school. Take turns to perform the activity.

Grammar Guide: Interesting language points

Here are some expressions used to ask for and give directions:

Asking for directions

How can I get to...

Could you please guide me to reach...

Could you show me the way to...

Could you tell me how to get to...

Where is...

What's the best way to get to...

Giving directions

Go straight till...

Turn left/right.

Take the first turn to the left/right.

Go past the...

The .... is beside/in front of/next to...

Communication Skills NEP

C2. *Role-play* — **Read the following conversation.**

Naman: Dad, please let me drive the car for a few minutes.

Father: I'm sorry, I can't. You're too young to drive.

Naman: Excuse me, that may be true of some people, but I am a very careful person. I'll drive carefully and follow all the rules.

Father: I know you are a very careful boy. But you are not allowed to drive without a driving licence. And you can't get a driving licence until you turn eighteen.

Naman: I know what you mean, but it should be okay if I drive only in the neighbourhood and don't go out.

Father: I'm afraid, we must follow the rules. I'm sure you understand that we can't break the law.

Manners matter!

Remember, even when we disagree with someone, we need not be rude. We should make our point politely.

Now, role-play a situation between Aarav and his mother. Aarav wants a mobile phone while his mother thinks he is too young to have a phone. As Aarav, justify your request with proper reasons.

Grammar Guide: Interesting language points

Here are some polite expressions used to interrupt others:

Excuse me…

Excuse me for interrupting but…

Pardon me,…

I'm afraid but…

Sorry to interrupt,…

I'm sorry…

Could I add something here?

Could I interrupt you for a moment please?

Do not use expressions such as the following:

Be quiet and listen to me.

Can't you be quiet for a moment?

Will you just shut up for a minute, please?

Shut your mouth and do what I say.

Didn't you hear what I said?

Saying it right

D1. *Listen and sort* 10.4

Listen to some words with the sounds a as in *cap* and a as in *bath*. Repeat the words and write them in the correct columns. Then, say them aloud.

Words with a as in *cap*	Words with a as in *bath*

D2. *Repeat and write* 10.5

Listen and repeat the words ending with ough. Then, write them down in the given space.

1. ______
2. ______
3. ______
4. ______
5. ______
6. ______
7. ______

Now, think of three more words ending with ough. Then, write them down in your notebook.

Dictation time

E. *Listen and write* DT

Listen to the passage and write it in your notebook. Then, take turns to read it out to your partner.

Interacting and communicating

Creativity NEP

F. *Interrupt and respond*

Read the situations given below. What would you say to interrupt someone in the situations and how would you respond? Work with a partner and role-play the situations.

Example:

Student: Excuse me, ma'am. May I have a minute of yours, please?

Teacher: Yes, please.

Situations

1. Your teacher is teaching a lesson but you need to go to the washroom urgently.
2. Your parents are having a serious conversation but you need to ask your mother something right now.
3. Your friends are having a debate about something and you want to give your opinion on it.
4. Your father is on a call but you need to ask him something urgent.

Grammar Guide: Interesting language points

Here are some expressions used to interrupt others and respond to interruptions:

Expressions used to interrupt	**Possible responses**
Actually…	*Yes, please…*
Excuse me…	*How can I…*
I'm sorry, but…	*No problem…*
I just want to say…	*Please…*
May I interrupt you here?	*Of course,…*
Do you mind if I say something?	*Please go ahead…*

Fun Activity

Experiential Learning NEP

Form groups of four students each. Blindfold one person from your group and instruct him/her to find a certain thing. It could be a tree, a swing, a chair, etc.

The blindfolded person will have to reach the place on the basis of the directions given to him/her by the group members. The success of the task will depend on how well the directions are given and comprehended.

Perform the activity in an open space. Ensure that the area is safe and does not have any dangerous objects nearby.

11 Science and technology

In this chapter, we will:

- learn to express our views and opinions.
- learn to discuss, contrast and compare situations.
- learn to order events on the basis of listening.
- learn to debate and talk about environmental changes.
- learn to say words with the digraph oo and the diphthong ow.
- learn to say words with the short o sound as in *lot* and the long o sound as in *told*.

15 LIFE ON LAND

Getting started

A. *Discuss*

Look at the pictures. These are some of the extinct animals and birds. What do you think leads to the extinction of a species? Research on the Internet and find out more about these species and the causes of their extinction.

The woolly mammoth

The tasmanian tiger

The dodo

The great auk

The passenger pigeon

Listening and learning

B1. *Gap-fill* 11.1

Listen to a news story about the simultaneous launch of 104 satellites by Indian Space Research Organisation (ISRO) and fill in the blanks in the news story below.

On the remarkable day of .... 2017, ISRO's (Indian Space Research Organisation) Polar Satellite Launch Vehicle (PSLV) successfully launched the .... along with .... co-passenger satellites, from .... Space Centre (SHAR), Sriharikota. It is considered to be the .... consecutively successful mission of PSLV. All the .... satellites carried on-board are said to weigh .... kilograms in totality.

The satellite was lifted off at .... a.m., as planned, from the First Launch Pad. The satellites achieved a polar Sun Orbit of .... kilometres after a flight of .... All the 104 satellites successfully separated from the PSLV fourth stage in a fixed sequence in the succeeding ....minutes. The total number of Indian satellites launched by PSLV now stands at ....

B2. *Order correctly* 11.2

Listen to a short biography of Dr Homi Jehangir Bhabha and number his life events in the correct order.

He denounced the use of atomic bombs and advocated peaceful use of atomic energy. ☐

In 1948, the Atomic Energy Commission was established and Bhabha was appointed its first director. ☐

Homi Jehangir Bhabha is known as the 'Father of the Indian nuclear programme'. ☐

He also represented India in the International Atomic Energy Agency conferences during the 1950s. ☐

He was born on 30th October 1909. His father was Jehangir Hormusji Bhabha, a well-known lawyer, and his mother was Maheren. ☐

After his death, the Atomic Energy Commission was renamed after him as the Bhabha Atomic Research Centre. ☐

In 1954, he established the Tata Institute of Fundamental Research. ☐

He studied at Cathedral and John Connon School, and at the age of 15 entered Elphinstone College. ☐

Going against his father's wish, who wanted him to become an engineer, Bhabha joined Cambridge University and shifted his interests to theoretical physics. ☐

He died in a plane crash near Mont Blanc on 24th January 1966. ☐

Speaking and practising

Critical Thinking NEP

C1. *Discuss*

Work with a partner and discuss whether life was better in the past or it is better now. Compare these two periods—the former with fewer gadgets and facilities and the latter with technologically advanced machines.

Word Wizard: Useful words and phrases

You can include the following words and phrases in your discussion:

blessings of science	employment
fast production	demerits
however	in comparison
by contrast	loss of agricultural land
similarly	on the other hand

Critical Thinking NEP

C2. *Debate*

Divide the class into groups and hold a debate on the motion 'Modern technology is a boon to mankind.'

Grammar Guide: Interesting language points

Here are some introductory phrases we use to express our views and to disagree with others' views politely:

I think...
I see what you mean but...
To my mind,...
I take the view that...
It seems to me that...
In my opinion...
I beg to disagree...
I agree with that but...
Sorry, but I disagree...
I'm afraid, I don't agree with that.

Saying it right

D1. *Repeat and write*

11.3

Digraph: A digraph is a combination of two letters representing a single sound. For example, *ph* in *phone* and *ey* in *key*.

Diphthong: A diphthong is a sound formed by the combination of two vowel sounds into a single syllable. The sound begins as one vowel and moves towards another, as in *coin*, *loud*, and *side*.

Listen and repeat the words with the digraph oo and the diphthong ow. Then, write them in the correct columns.

Words with oo sound	Words with ow sound
____________	____________
____________	____________
____________	____________
____________	____________
____________	____________
____________	____________
____________	____________
____________	____________

D2. *Sort*

11.4

Listen, repeat and circle the words with the short o sound as in *lot* and underline the words with the long o sound as in *told*.

hot	rope	stock	clock
clot	allot	coast	cannot
cope	got	flock	smock
brought	hope	block	slot
most	frock	sock	talk

Dictation time

E. *Listen and write*

DT

Listen to the passage and write it in your notebook. Then, take turns to read it out to your partner.

13 CLIMATE ACTION

Interacting and communicating

F. *Ask and answer*

Watch a PowerPoint presentation on global warming. Work with a partner, take turns and ask and answer the following questions.

1. What is global warming?
2. What are the effects of global warming?
3. What are the main causes of global warming?
4. What, according to you, can be done to check global warming?
5. Discuss the consequences of global warming.

12 RESPONSIBLE CONSUMPTION AND PRODUCTION

Fun Activity

Managing and recycling plastic waste is an environmental issue faced by the entire planet today. How can you contribute towards the management, recycling, and eradication of plastic waste? Work as groups and think of creative ways to recycle plastic waste. You may either use your school library or the Internet to research on this topic. Helpful topics to search on could be:

- the effects of plastic waste on our planet.
- the three Rs: reduce, reuse and recycle.
- microorganisms and their role in eliminating plastic waste.

Present your research as a PowerPoint presentation not exceeding ten minutes.

12 What's in store for us?

In this chapter, we will:

- learn to talk about various environmental concerns and share our opinions on them.
- learn to listen to and comprehend speeches and poems.
- learn to suggest ways to solve problems.
- learn to say words ending in ing and ink sounds.

13 CLIMATE ACTION

Getting started

A. *Discuss*

Watch a PowerPoint presentation on pollution. Then, work with a partner and discuss the following points.

1. Whose responsibility do you think it is to protect the environment?
2. What can we do to we save water?
3. Suggest some ways of reducing our electricity consumption.
4. Suggest one thing to reduce the consumption of petroleum and emission of carbon dioxide.

Listening and learning

B1. *Gap-fill*

12.1

Listen to an extract from a speech delivered at the Rio Earth Summit 1992, by the twelve-year-old Severn Suzuki of Canada. Listen carefully and complete the extract.

13 CLIMATE ACTION

Hello, I'm Severn Suzuki, speaking for ECO: the Environmental Children's Organization. We are a group of twelve- and thirteen-year olds trying to make a .... Vanessa Suttie, Morgan Geisler, Michelle Quigg and me. We raised all the .... to come here ourselves, to come .... miles to tell you adults you must change your ways.

Coming up here today, I have no hidden agenda. I am fighting for my future. Losing my future is not like losing an election or a few points on the stock market. I am here to speak for all generations to come. I am here to speak on behalf of the .... around the world whose cries go unheard. I am here to speak for the .... dying across this planet because they have nowhere left to go. I am afraid to go out in the sun now because of the .... in our ozone. I am afraid to breathe the air because I don't know what .... are in it. I used to go fishing in Vancouver, my home, with my dad until just a few years ago we found the fish full of .... And now we hear of animals and plants going extinct every day—vanishing forever.

In my life, I have dreamt of seeing the great herds of wild animals, jungles and rainforests full of birds and butterflies, but now I wonder if they will even exist for my children to see. Did you have to worry of these things when you were my age? All this is happening before our eyes and yet we act as if we have all the time we want and all the .... I'm only a child and I don't have all the solutions, but I want you to realize, neither do you... You don't know how to fix the holes in our ozone layer, you don't know how to bring the salmon back up a dead stream. You don't know how to bring back an animal now extinct. And you can't bring back the .... that once grew where there is now .... If you don't know how fix it, please stop breaking it!

B2. *Write and check* (12.2)

Listen to a short poem about what the world would be like when it will stop raining. Listen to it again and as you listen, write it down. Listen for the third time and check if you wrote it correctly.

13 CLIMATE ACTION

Speaking and practising

C1. *Deliver a speech*

Read this short excerpt about our natural world written by Tenzin Gyatso, the fourteenth Dalai Lama.

The Natural World

If there is one area in which both education and the media have a special responsibility, it is, I believe, our natural environment. This responsibility has less to do with questions of right or wrong than with the question of survival. The natural world is our home.

It is therefore in our interest to look after it. This is common sense. But only recently have the size of our population and the power of science and technology grown to the point that they have a direct impact on nature. The problems caused by environmental disasters can be seen as her response to our irresponsible behaviour. She is warning us that there are limits.

As a young man, I recall seeing great numbers of different species whenever I travelled outside Lhasa. My chief memory of the three-month journey across Tibet from my birthplace at Takster in the East to Lhasa, is of the wildlife we encountered along the way.

Immense herds of *kiang* (wild asses) and *drong* (wild yak) freely roamed the great plains. Occasionally we would catch sight of shimmering herds of *gowa*, the shy Tibetan gazelle, of *wa*, the white-lipped deer, or of *tso*, our majestic antelope. I remember, too, my fascination for the little *chibi*, or *pika*, which would congregate on grassy areas. They were so friendly. I loved to watch the birds: the dignified *gho* (the bearded eagle) soaring high above monasteries and perched up in the mountains; the flocks of *nangbar* (geese); and occasionally, at night, to hear the call of the *wookpa* (the long-eared owl).

Sadly, this profusion of wildlife is no longer to be found. Partly due to hunting but primarily due to loss of habitat. Whereas before wild animals would often come close to the house, today they are hardly anywhere to be seen.

Equally troubling is the devastation of Tibet's forests. In the past, the hills were all thickly wooded; today those who have been back report that they are clean-shaven. We cannot say for sure what the ultimate effects of, for example, deforestation might be on the soil and the local rainfall, let alone what the implications are for the planet's weather systems. The only clear thing is that we humans are the only species with the power to destroy the earth as we know it.

The birds have no such power, nor do the insects, nor does any mammal. Yet if we have the capacity to destroy the earth, so, too, do we have the capacity to protect it. More and more people have now started expressing concern about the environmental changes.

Form groups, discuss the changes brought about in the world by environmental changes and make a list of them. For example, there are fewer trees, some animals or birds can't be seen anymore, some plants no longer grow. Then, give a speech on the subject in class.

Grammar Guide: Interesting language points

Here are some expressions you can use to introduce your ideas:

I am most concerned about...	*I am upset about...*
What bothers me is that...	*I feel very bad about...*
I am scared to think...	*It is terrible to think that...*

Creativity • Critical Thinking NEP

C2. *Discuss* **Work in pairs. Discuss and plan what you can do to solve environmental problems in your neighbourhood. It could be checking the levels of air, water or noise.**

Example:

Sanjay: How can we solve the problem of air pollution in the city?

Ajay: If we all do our bit, we can solve it without much difficulty.

Sanjay: What do you suggest doing?

Ajay: Why don't we all plant trees in our neighbourhood?

Grammar Guide: Interesting language points

Here are some expressions you can use to ask for and give suggestions:

What can we...	*I think we can...*
Why don't we...	*I'm sure we can...*
What would you suggest...	*I think it's possible if we all...*

Saying it right

D1. *Circle*

Listen to the sentences and circle the correct word.

1. She played/play very well.
2. They clean/cleaned the house.
3. We need/needed some pencils
4. They cook/cooked great food.
5. They arrive/arrived early morning.
6. My parents listened/listen to soft music.
7. The old women walk/walked carefully.
8. We talked/talk on the phone.

D2. *Repeat and write*

Listen to some words, and repeat and write them correctly.

____________	____________	____________
____________	____________	____________
____________	____________	____________

Dictation time

E. *Listen and write*

Listen to the passage and write it in your notebook. Then, take turns to read it out to your partner.

11 SUSTAINABLE CITIES AND COMMUNITIES

Interacting and communicating

F. *Discuss* 12.5

Listen to a news story about how Sweden disposes its waste. Then find out how and where waste is disposed of in our country.

Talk about the methods in the class and discuss if they are the right ways of disposing waste. You can also talk about their advantages or disadvantages.

Fun Activity

13 CLIMATE ACTION

Use the Internet and find out the complete speech of Severn Suzuki that she delivered at Rio Earth Summit 1992. Then discuss how you feel about the reaction of the people present at the summit.

13 Arts and crafts

In this chapter, we will:

- learn to talk about arts and crafts.
- learn to describe processes and appreciate arts and crafts.
- learn to create awareness about different issues.
- learn to prepare and present reports.
- learn to divide words into syllables.

Getting started

India Focus NEP

A. *Discuss* 13.1

Have you ever seen a puppet show? Listen to the story behind this traditional puppet show and fill in the blanks.

The traditional .... play of Rajasthan is known by the name of .... (play of Amar Singh Rathore).

Amar Singh Rathore belonged to the royal family of .... state and was the .... son of Gaj Singh. He was the natural .... of the king, but the king was angry with him and he appointed the younger brother .... as his heir-apparent.

Amar Singh was given the .... area in Marwar which was under the central rule of the .... Due to his .... to the Emperor, he served as one of the important courtiers of the Mughal court. But due to his .... and ...., he did not get along with ...., who was the Mughal Emperor's brother and his trustworthy courtier.

The .... between the two grew to the extent that one day Amar Singh found an opportunity to slay .... in open court and in the presence of the Emperor. Total .... ensued and everyone ran to save their lives.

Emperor Shah Jahan found it difficult to .... Amar Singh. Therefore, he employed ...., brother-in-law of Amar Singh, and conspired with him to kill Amar Singh. One day, Arjun Gaur found an opportunity to bring Amar Singh to the court and .... him in the back.

Due to the fear of the ....,
Amar Singh's dead body was kept under guard at .... and nobody was allowed to take it to Nagaur for cremation. Finally, Amar Singh's nephew .... bravely fought the Mughal soldiers and took his uncle's body home.

Listening and learning

India Focus NEP

B1. *Order correctly* 13.2

Listen to how we make a traditional Rajasthani puppet. Then, number the sentences in the correct order.

a. Take the wooden rod and tie pieces of cloth on it with thread. ☐

b. Paint the face. Draw a moustache for the king and long hair for the queen. Leave the faces to dry. ☐

c. Cut the thermocol or piece of wood in the shape of a face. It should look roughly like a face but need not look exactly like one. ☐

d. Now, decorate the clothes of the king and queen with your decorating material. Your puppets are ready. ☐

e. Cover the chest and arms with colorful clothes. You could paste or staple the clothes. ☐

f. To present a story through your puppets, you will have to make them dance! To do this, attach threads from both the hands and legs (4 threads each) to a wooden cross section (two rods of wood at 90 degrees to each other). By moving these wooden pieces up and down – your puppets will dance in the air. Enjoy! ☐

g. Make small holes at the bottom of the faces and insert some part of the wooden rod into it. The face should stand on the rod. The rest of rod will be the chest of the puppet. ☐

B2. *Gap-fill*

13.3

Listen carefully to a radio announcement about an art and craft fair and complete the brochure below.

Fine Arts Society

.... of Engineers presents

Dharohar

Arts and Crafts Mela

on Saturday, 14 October 2017

from .... at IIE, Delhi campus.

Attractive prizes and .... to be won!

Fashion show

Design your own .... and walk the ramp.

....

Let your face be painted in beautiful colours by great artists.

....

A calligraphy workshop by ....

Speaking and practising

C1. *Give a presentation*

Read the following article about the dying crafts in our country.

After agriculture, handicraft is the second largest occupation in India. India is one of the very few countries in the world that have a tradition of handicrafts dating back to over 5000 years. Rajasthan is famous for its pottery and marble handicrafts while UP, Tamil Nadu and Delhi have earned a worldwide recognition for their handmade jewellery and woodcrafts.

For centuries, these were worshipped arts whose secrets weren't revealed to the outside world. The skills would be passed down from generation to generation and that is how every region acquired their unique art form. However, modernisation and increasing use of machines is threatening local handicraft.

Handmade goods take months to produce but machines produce them faster and at a lower cost. Buyers are attracted to low-priced items produced by machines. And then there is lack of awareness about handicrafts in people. Artisans are not often able to make a living from their craftsmanship. Many artisans are now leaving their crafts to make a living in other fields.

Now, form groups and discuss what you can do to promote the crafts of your region. Would you organise an exhibition/a workshop, or help raise awareness of the products?

Think of innovative ways to promote local goods and make a presentation with the help of a brochure or poster.

C2. *Discuss*

Work with a partner, take turns and ask and answer the following questions. Remember that films, music, painting, sculpture and dance are all forms of art.

1. Do you like to draw or paint?
2. Do you think you are a good artist?
3. Have you ever been to an art exhibition or a crafts market?
4. Can anyone be an artist, or do we need to have a special talent for it?
5. Do you think all children should be taught art in school?
6. Do you have any art pieces or local handicraft at home? If yes, describe them.
7. What kind of art is your state famous for?
8. Do your parents encourage you to take up any art?

Saying it right

D1. *Count syllables* 13.4

Listen to the following words and repeat them. Also divide their syllables and write the number of syllables each word has.

Word	Syllable break-up	No. of syllables
Monday	Mon/day	2
dog		
green		
basket		
quiet		
orange		
table		
expensive		
interesting		
unrealistic		

D2. *Repeat and underline* 13.5

Listen, repeat and underline the word that you hear in each set of words.

1. fit/fat/foul
2. get/got/good
3. mad/made/main
4. sat/sell/set
5. good/food/foot
6. bet/bat/bait
7. shell/shall/short
8. jail/jazz/joy
9. see/sip/sack
10. doll/dull/dip

Dictation time

E. *Listen and write*

Listen to the passage and write it in your notebook. Then, take turns to read it out to your partner.

DT

Interacting and communicating

Experiential Learning NEP

F. *Present a report*

Visit an art exhibition, a crafts mela or a handicraft unit in your town. Find out about the works of art and craft, the artists and the processes used in making and selling their products. Write a report and present it to the class.

Fun Activity

Creativity • Art Integration NEP

Decorate your class with various works of art. You may put up paintings, sculptures, pictures of popular artists and write-ups about them. Then, organise a class exhibition and invite students of others classes. Tell them about your artworks.

Saying it better!

Common mistakes	Use this instead
When asking about someone: How's you?	How are you? How're you? (How's you is never used to greet or ask about someone, even informally.)
When writing an email, message or letter: Using only "Dear" at the starting	Dear .... (name, sometimes with the addition of Mr or Ms when addressed to an adult) (Using only Dear is an incorrect way of greeting someone in email, message or letter.)
When introducing oneself: Myself Avinash.	Hi/Hello, I am .... (name). (A reflexive or emphasising pronoun is never used to begin one's introduction).
When talking about one's school or class: I read in .... (school or class & section)	I study in .... (first mention your class and section), in .... (then your school's full name)
When asking the price of something: How much? Or How much is the cost?	What is the price of this item? Or How much does this cost?

When asking someone where he/ she is from: Where do you put up?	Where are you from? Or Where do you live? (Where do you put up should only be used when someone is staying temporarily at a place, like in a hotel)
When using wanna or gonna I wanna paint. Or I'm gonna do my work later.	Wanna and gonna are short forms of *want to* and *going to*. They should be used in informal conversation **only**.
Over- or Incorrect use of literally Jayant was literally smiling on his birthday. Or It was literally raining cats and dogs.	Jayant was smiling happily on his birthday. It was raining cats and dogs. (Literally, as an expression, should only be used when an action is otherwise only figuratively possible.)
Over- or incorrect use of like: Lalitha was like so happy, that she was like screaming with like so much joy.	Lalitha was so happy that she was screaming with joy. (Like is always used as a simile and never as a punctuation.) His hair was black like storm clouds.

Common phrases

Do you know what small talk is? It is polite conversation about unimportant things. People make small talk at social occasions. It is generally used as a conversation starter or an ice-breaker with an unfamiliar person or a group of people.

Here are a few ways of engaging in small talk. You will notice that information about general themes is being used here.

It's so gloomy, it feels like inside an upside-down fishbowl.
Yes, it's horribly muggy.
The traffic was terrible today.
I hear that they are closing off a few roads for the pipeline construction.
Do you use the metro?
Yes, it's so convenient.

Did you hear about the crisis in Ukraine?
Yes, I was reading about it in the newspaper yesterday.
I think I might go to the Lit Fest this weekend. Are you planning to go there too?
No. Could you tell me more about this Lit Fest? It sounds interesting.

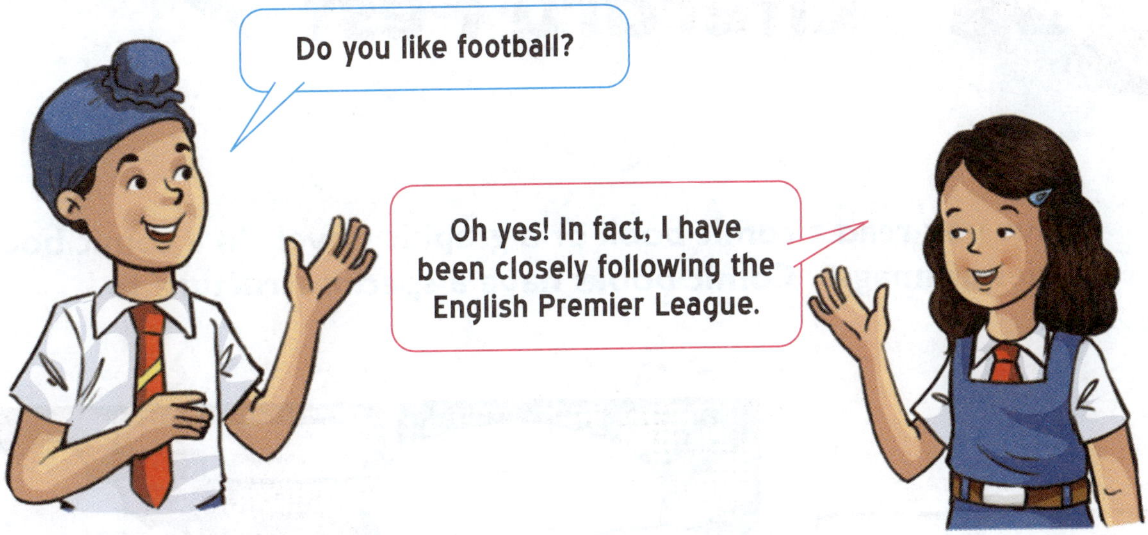
Do you like football?
Oh yes! In fact, I have been closely following the English Premier League.

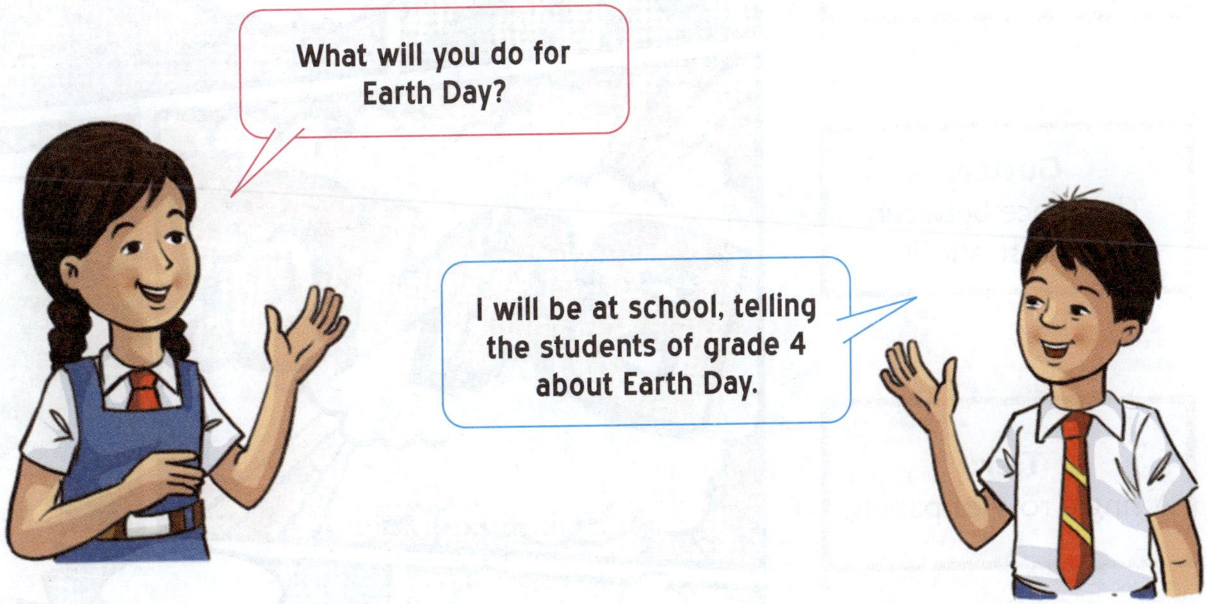
What will you do for Earth Day?
I will be at school, telling the students of grade 4 about Earth Day.

Children's Literary Fest

Have you read a comic book or a graphic novel? In a comic book, series of images. Comic books have a special structure to

Panel:
A single illustration with borders.

Gutter:
The space between the illustrations.

Tier:
A single row of panels.

Spread:
An illustration spread over two facing pages.

the story is conveyed not only through words but also through a lay the story out for readers. A single page has important features like:

Splash:
A full-page illustration that draws attention to the most important mood or action.

Caption:
A box providing the context through the narrator's voice.

Speech bubble:
These contain the dialogues, with a 'tail' pointing to the speaker. A wavy/cloudy bubble generally denotes dreams or thoughts while oval bubbles are dialogues.

Select your favourite story from the ones that you have read. Reproduce a scene from that story as a comic in the space given below.

Notes

Notes

Notes